Gluten-Free French Desserts and Baked Goods

Published in the U.S. by
Book Publishing Company
415 Farm Road
P.O. Box 99
Summertown, TN 38483
888-260-8458
www.bookpubco.com

Printed in Hong Kong

ISBN-13 978-1-57067-187-6
ISBN-10 1-57067-187-7

14 13 12 11 10 09 08 07 06   1 2 3 4 5 6 7 8 9

Originally published as *Desserts et Pains Sans Gluten*
© Éditions La Plage, 2004

Cupillard, Valerie.
  [Desserts et pains sans gluten English]
  Gluten-free French desserts and baked goods / recipes by Valerie Cupillard ; photos by Philippe
Barret and Myriam Gauthier-Moreau.
      p. cm.
  "Originally published as Desserts et Pains Sans Gluten editions La Plage, 2004."--T.p. verso.
  Includes index.
  ISBN-13: 978-1-57067-187-6
  ISBN-10: 1-57067-187-7
  1. Gluten-free diet--Recipes. 2. Cookery, French. 3. Desserts. 4. Baking. I. Barret, Philippe. II.
Gauthier-Moreau, Myriam. III. Title.

  RM237.86.C86 2006
  641.5'638--dc22   2006004844

Gluten-Free

FRENCH DESSERTS AND BAKED GOODS

Recipes by Valérie Cupillard ▪ Photos by Philippe Barret and Myriam Gauthier-Moreau

Book Publishing Company
Summertown, Tennessee

Photographer and gourmet Philippe Barret lives and works in the Drôme. He has illustrated numerous books and collaborated on diverse publications displaying the recipes of the greatest chefs of cooking and pastry.

A young photographer passionate about cuisine and organic foods, Myriam Gauthier-Moreau has participated in many works of this type. From the preparation of the recipes to the final presentation, she enjoys immersing herself in this world of tastes, textures, and colors.

For Michèle:
For the small moments of happiness
and the snacks at the farm.

Introduction

Eliminating gluten from the diet is a tremendous change. Wheat flour is omnipresent in all the classic baked goods, and we are seldom in the habit of using other ingredients. And yet gluten is absent in rice, soy, buckwheat, tapioca, millet, quinoa, amaranth, chestnuts, almonds, hazelnuts, coconut, and an endless number of other foods that can be used to make fabulous desserts and breads. Many of these ingredients are available in a variety forms, such as flours, flakes, and finely ground powders. By incorporating these ingredients, you will have an opportunity to transform a "diet" into a wonderful gourmet discovery!

With this book I offer you a new way to approach the world of desserts. Enjoy Lemon Brioche (page 30), made with millet semolina, or Peach Crumble with Crunchy Rice Topping (page 84). These recipes provide a great wealth of flavors that, when blended with a little imagination, will allow you to easily prepare tasty and original desserts.

The basic ingredients for these recipes are healthful and simple: rice flour in the light Tropical Sponge Cake (page 36) and Orange Caramel Cake (page 46); quinoa flour in Chocolate Cake Impérial (page 38); finely ground almonds in Autumn Shortbread Cookies (page 104); chestnut flour in Chestnut Flour Clafoutis (page 75); fine rice semolina in Yogurt Cake (page 52). These ingredients will help you follow a sweetly pleasurable and imaginative diet that will tempt your family and introduce new flavors to your guests.

Valérie Cupillard

Award-winning author of numerous cookbooks, Valérie Cupillard develops recipes blending gastronomy and dietary concerns. She enlivens conferences and workshops by introducing a new cuisine that is healthful and organic.

Find out more about Valérie on her Web site:
www.biogourmand.com

Other books by Valérie Cupillard

By La Plage Publishing:
Eat Less Sugar
Gluten-free, Naturally
Oils, Balancing Omega-6/ Omega-3
Without Milk and Without Eggs

Cereals and Legumes
Germinated Grains
Organic Breakfasts
Organic Desserts: Healthy Treats as the Seasons Go By
Organic Feasts: Entertain as the Seasons Go By
Organic Sauces
Organic Soups: Season by Season
Quinoa
Unique Vegetarian Dishes

Contents

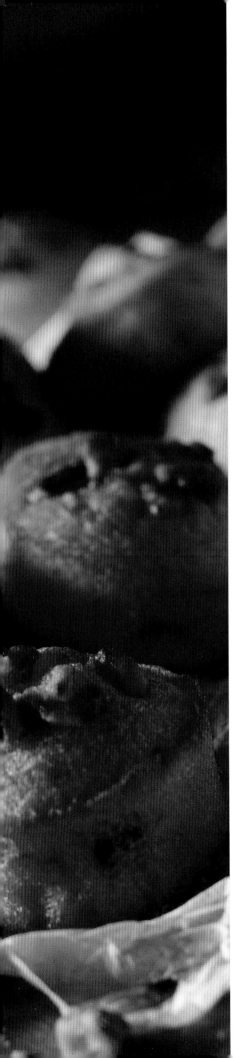

Precautions

People suffering from celiac disease should take care to read labels and verify the ingredients they purchase in order to detect the presence of gluten. Unless you possess a grain mill, you should contact the manufacturer to verify that the rice flour (for example) comes from a mill reserved for this use only, and not from a mill that also grinds wheat, in order to protect yourself from all traces of gluten. Pay attention as well to the composition of chocolate, powdered sugar, and finely ground nut products, which can contain wheat flour. Wheat flour can also be found in dried fruits like figs or dates, which are sometimes powdered, and certain spice mixes (chili powder or curry powder, for example). Check the ingredients of nondairy milks; some brands may be mixed with grain milks that contain gluten (oat milk, for example). Adapt the recipes and ideas in this book according to your intolerance, medical advice, and treatment you follow.

How to flavor naturally

Use only organic essential oils, authentically pure and natural, without preservatives or coloring. Organic essential oils are obtained from the by-products (millers offals) of plants that are cultivated without artificial fertilizers or synthetic pesticides, and they are extracted without the use of descaling agents or chemical solvents. During distillation the essential oil is obtained as well as the "floral water." The use of natural essential oils, in small doses, provides subtle touches of aroma. Three to six drops are enough to flavor a cake batter.

Hypotoxic diet

People who turn toward a gluten-free diet in order to follow Dr. Seignalet's hypotoxic regimen[1] will find here (in the continuation of my first work on the subject[2]) the same characteristics. My recipes are prepared exclusively with plant milks; there's not a single milk product of animal origin, as well as no cream or butter, and all genetically modified grains are avoided. The baking temperature of the cakes is as low as possible to obtain a good-tasting result.

1. Jean Seignalet, *L'alimentation ou la Troisième Médicine*, 3rd edition, Collection Écologie Humaine (Paris: François-Xavier de Guibert, 1998).
2. Valérie Cupillard, *Sans Gluten Naturellement* (Paris: La Plage Publications, 2002).

Instructions

- All the ingredients used in the recipes are easily found in natural food stores or co-ops.
- The baking powder used is not the traditional "baking powder"; it's a baking powder without gluten or phosphates, based on the fermentation of grapes and cornstarch, for example.
- For recipes that call for margarine, use dairy-free, non-hydrogenated vegetable margarine.
- Be sure to choose whole brown rice flour and not cream of rice, which is precooked. The result after baking isn't the same! (The clafoutis, for example, would be dense.)
- Unless stated otherwise, each recipe makes four servings.

Baking

- Unless indicated otherwise, you do not need to preheat the oven for the recipes.

Note: In my recipes I have chosen to avoid milk products in favor of all-vegetable alternatives. However, you will still have success if you choose to use cows' milk in the same proportions as the directions specify for vegetable milk.

Breads

Making bread ...

Naturally gluten-free flours

Gluten is absent in rice, buckwheat, quinoa, corn, and millet. Though most of the flours found in natural food stores are suitable for the majority of people with gluten intolerance, those suffering from celiac disease need to take extra precautions and verify all ingredients before purchasing a product in order to determine the presence of gluten. This is especially important when it comes to flour. In order to protect yourself from all traces of gluten, contact the manufacturer to verify that the flour comes from a mill that is used only for gluten-free flours and not from a mill that is also used for grinding wheat. According to your degree of gluten intolerance, as well as the medical advice and treatment you follow, you may want to consider purchasing a grain mill so you can grind your own grains.

Which flours should you choose for making bread?

I use rice flour as the primary flour for my bread doughs. Used alone it is somewhat dense and bland. You can take advantage of the subtle flavor of rice flour by blending it with other gluten-free flours, such as millet, quinoa, buckwheat, or chestnut. All these flours have a much more pronounced flavor, and when used individually they can make a rather heavy dough. For a more inter-esting texture and flavor, try adding flaked buckwheat, millet, or quinoa to gluten-free breads, or add seeds like sesame or sunflower. Fine rice or millet semolina, or whole or ground quinoa or amaranth, are good additions that will give more body to a dough based on rice flour; they will also help you obtain a tasty crumb.

... without gluten

What leavening should you use?

For making all the breads in this book, use a gluten-free baking powder (the same kind that you would use for cakes), but take care to verify the ingredients. The leavening called for in these recipes is not the traditional baking powder. It's a baking powder without gluten or phosphates, with a base of grape and cornstarch fermentation, for example.

Characteristics of gluten-free bread dough

Gluten-free bread doughs do not require kneading. However, it is necessary to maintain a very pliable consistency, which, in conjunction with baking powder, will help the bread rise more easily. Because bread dough based on gluten-free flours is, by necessity, very soft, it is impossible to form it into a traditional round loaf, so it must be baked as a rather flat loaf. To do this, choose a cake pan that will keep the loaf in a round shape (you can also use a pie pan). To make small individual loaves, pour the dough into mini pans.

Avoid baking gluten-free bread in a loaf pan, as that will make a thick bread with a compact crumb; instead, favor flatter pans, such as those used to make flat breads like focaccia.

Breads based on rice flour will not keep long; they are best served the same day or the next. Since they are prepared in just a few minutes, you have the advantage of enjoying fresh bread more frequently.

Quinoa Bread
with Currants   >

Almonds and currants make this bread the ideal accompaniment to salads, crudités, hummus, and vegetable purées. Whole quinoa is mixed into the rice and buckwheat flours. The quinoa grains expand during baking, adding air to the dough and giving a lighter body to the bread. A well-oiled pan will allow you to obtain a crispy crust.

1 cup rice flour

½ cup slivered almonds or chopped walnuts

7 tablespoons buckwheat flour

3 tablespoons currants

2 tablespoons quinoa

2 teaspoons baking powder

¾ teaspoon salt

1 cup water

■ Combine the rice flour, almonds, buckwheat flour, currants, quinoa, baking powder, and salt in a bowl. Pour in the water and mix vigorously. Pour immediately into a layer cake pan coated with olive oil. The dough will be quite soft and will spread out like a biscuit or shortbread.

■ Bake at 425 degrees Fahrenheit for 25 to 30 minutes. Halfway through the baking, brush the top of the bread with olive oil, which will help the crust to lightly brown.

■ After baking, turn the loaf out onto a cooling rack. This bread is delicious when served the same day or while still warm.

Sunflower Seed
and Amaranth Loaf

It takes barely thirty minutes to prepare and bake this round loaf. You can put it in the oven just before a meal and enjoy it while it's still warm in order to appreciate the crispness of the amaranth grains and the crust browned with olive oil.

1⅓ cups rice flour

2½ tablespoons sunflower seeds

2 tablespoons amaranth

2 teaspoons baking powder

¾ teaspoon salt

¾ cup water

■ Combine the rice flour, sunflower seeds, amaranth, baking powder, and salt in a bowl. Add the water and stir the dough rapidly. Turn out immediately onto a baking sheet or pie pan coated with olive oil. The dough will be quite soft and will practically spread itself out into a round loaf approximately 8 inches in diameter.

■ Bake at 400 degrees Fahrenheit for 25 minutes. The top crust will remain quite white. Halfway through baking you can brush the loaf with olive oil to brown the crust. An easier way, however, is to flip the loaf over after it has finished baking so that the side that baked against the oiled pan is now on top and is a crisp golden brown.

< Three Seed Bread with Millet

1/3 cup sunflower seeds

2 tablespoons sesame seeds

1 tablespoon poppy seeds

1 1/3 cups rice flour

2/3 cup fine millet semolina

4 teaspoons baking powder

3/4 teaspoon salt

1 cup water

This dough, based on rice flour and millet semolina, remains quite white after baking, yet the side that soaks up a little olive oil becomes brown and crusty. That's why this round loaf of grainy bread is served like a tatin: upside down!

■ Oil a 10-inch layer cake pan or pie pan with olive oil. Combine the sunflower seeds, sesame seeds, and poppy seeds in a small bowl. Sprinkle them over the bottom of the prepared pan.

■ Combine the rice flour, millet semolina, baking powder, and salt in a bowl. Add the water, stirring constantly and rapidly. The dough should be quite stiff and a little puffy.

■ Drop the dough over the seeds by spoonfuls so they touch. As the dough is soft, it will spread out as it bakes, making a round loaf. Bake at 400 degrees Fahrenheit for 25 minutes. Remove the bread from the oven and turn it out of the pan, seed side up.

Chestnut Mini Loaves with Hazelnuts >>

1 1/3 cups rice flour

1 cup chestnut flour

2 1/2 teaspoons baking powder

3/4 teaspoon salt

3/4 cup water

6 tablespoons coarsely chopped hazelnuts

Note: This recipe makes 6 mini loaves.

These small loaves have a very sweet flavor thanks to the chestnut flour, which gives them an almost sugary taste. Enjoy them warm when they first come out of the oven.

■ Combine the rice flour, chestnut flour, baking powder, and salt in a bowl. Add the water, stirring constantly. The dough will appear frothy and will begin to rise.

■ With damp hands and the aid of a spatula, form the dough into tangerine-sized, slightly elongated balls. Arrange the loaves on a baking sheet lined with parchment paper, spacing them evenly apart. Sprinkle 1 tablespoon of the hazelnuts on each loaf, pressing them on gently to help them stick to the dough. Bake at 400 degrees Fahrenheit for 20 minutes. The surface of the loaves should become cracked.

Note: For a slightly golden color, quickly remove the baking sheet from the oven after about 15 minutes of baking and brush the tops of the mini loaves with a brush dipped in olive oil; immediately return the loaves to the oven to bake for another 5 minutes.

Chestnut Mini Loaves
with Hazelnuts

< Quinoa Bread with Turmeric

2/3 cup rice flour
6 tablespoons quinoa
1 teaspoon baking powder
Heaping 1/4 teaspoon salt
2 pinches turmeric
3/4 cup water

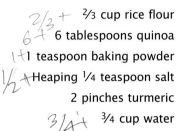

Quinoa gives a pleasing crumb to this bread, which is faintly tinged yellow due to turmeric. This is a good bread to accompany salads, crudités, and sautéed legumes.

■ Combine the rice flour, quinoa, baking powder, salt, and turmeric in a bowl. Add the water, stirring constantly, to make a thin dough. Pour the dough into an oiled layer cake pan. The pan should only be filled halfway.

■ Bake at 425 degrees Fahrenheit for about 25 minutes. Remove the bread from the pan while it is warm, and let it cool completely. The quinoa will continue to expand and absorb moisture as the bread cools.

Steam-Baked Loaves >>

2/3 cup rice flour
1 tablespoon amaranth
4 teaspoons sunflower seeds
1 teaspoon baking powder
Heaping 1/4 teaspoon salt
Scant 1/2 cup water

You can successfully make these small loaves even without an oven. This recipe uses the same dough as the Sunflower Seed and Amaranth Loaf (page 12), but it is divided into small portions and cooked by gentle steam. This will fill five ramekins placed in a standard-size steamer.

■ Coat 5 glass ramekins with olive oil. Combine the rice flour, amaranth, sunflower seeds, baking powder, and salt in a bowl. Add the water and stir the dough rapidly. Divide the dough equally among the ramekins, but don't fill them more than halfway so the dough can expand.

■ Arrange the ramekins in a steamer basket in a heavy-bottomed saucepan and steam gently over low heat for 20 to 25 minutes. Be careful that the condensation on the lid doesn't fall onto the loaves and make them wet.

■ You can remove the loaves from the ramekins when they are warm, or serve them while still in the molds.

Steam-Baked Loaves

< Olive Focaccia

¾ cup fine rice semolina
⅔ cup rice flour
1 teaspoon baking powder
¾ teaspoon salt
½ cup water
¼ cup olive oil
1 cup pitted black olives
1 pinch dried thyme
or rosemary

Plenty of olives enrich this bun-like dough.

■ Combine the rice semolina, rice flour, baking powder, and salt in a bowl. Add the water and oil all at once, stirring constantly. Add the black olives and thyme, mixing the dough a little with a spatula.

■ Spoon the dough into a layer cake pan coated with olive oil. With slightly moistened hands, form the dough into a round loaf. Bake at 425 degrees Fahrenheit for 25 minutes. Halfway through the baking you can quickly remove the focaccia from the oven to brush a little olive oil across the top, if desired.

Sesame Focaccia: Reduce the olives to ½ cup and add 2½ tablespoons sesame seeds.

Pizza Dough

1⅓ cups rice flour
2 teaspoons baking powder
2 pinches salt
¾ cup water
Pizza sauce and toppings
of your choice

This is a soft pizza dough that isn't kneaded. It's simply poured into a pie pan lined with parchment paper (indispensable!) and prebaked before spreading on the toppings.

■ Combine the flour, baking powder, and salt in a bowl. Pour in the water, stirring rapidly. With the aid of a spatula, spread the dough in a large pie pan lined with parchment paper. The dough should be a little less than ½ inch thick.

■ Bake at 425 degrees Fahrenheit for 10 minutes. Remove the crust from the oven and spread it immediately with a thick tomato pizza sauce and the toppings of your choice without going all the way to the edge. Raise the oven temperature to 450 degrees Fahrenheit. Return the pizza to the oven, and bake it for 20 minutes longer.

Pastry Crust

Very easy to shape, this pastry crust complements savory fillings, quiches, or vegetable pies.

■ Place all the ingredients in a food processor and process until well combined. Add 1 to 2 tablespoons of water, if needed, so the mixture sticks together and forms a ball of dough.

■ Knead the dough lightly, then place it on a pastry board dusted with rice flour. Roll it out with a floured rolling pin.

■ Line a pie pan with the crust and pour your quiche filling directly into it, or prebake the crust if you are going to fill it with precooked vegetables in a béchamel sauce.

3/4 cup quinoa flour

2/3 cup rice flour

2 eggs

4 tablespoons olive oil

1 teaspoon baking powder

3/4 teaspoon salt

Brioches

Making brioches ...

Which flours should you choose to make brioches?

Just as for the bread doughs, the basic flour to favor is rice flour. You can combine it with fine millet or rice semolina, which will transform the texture of the dough and give it a more brioche-like consistency. Without yeast, this brioche dough rises instantly, due to the addition of baking powder.

How to flavor brioche batter

Orange flower water is delicate and unassuming, a flavor that harmonizes well both with the other components of the brioche and with whatever you might add to it. Slices of a brioche flavored with orange flower water can be spread with fruit marmalade or honey.

If you wish to flavor your brioche with an essential oil, choose an organic one and select only a citrus fruit essential oil. Measure precisely, and add only three to six drops of lemon, bergamot, or grapefruit essential oil to the batter, which will give it an agreeable aroma and flavor. Consider grating an orange or lemon peel so you can add the flavorful zest to the batter. A brioche will also be excellent with a few anise seeds or pinches of ground cinnamon.

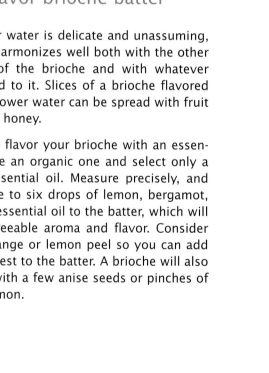

... without gluten

What kind of fat should you use?

Vegetable margarine (non-hydrogenated and organic) provides an easily blended basic fat to combine with sugar to make a creamy mixture, while light olive oil is suitable for a batter that contains a fine semolina (rice or millet). Contrary to what you might think, the flavor of the olive oil is scarcely noticeable once the batter is baked, remaining very subtle. If you appreciate this healthful alternative, you can keep a bottle of light olive oil flavored with vanilla for your baked goods. Let an already scraped and used vanilla bean pod soak in it; that will be sufficient to impart a delicate flavor. Wait a few weeks before using. Alternatively, to have it available more quickly, you can obtain the seeds from a vanilla bean pod and add them to the oil, or put in several pinches of grated vanilla.

How to sweeten

If you choose to sweeten the batter with organic dark brown sugar, the sugar will impart all of its aroma and flavor and be perfectly sufficient. If you would rather flavor with an essential oil or orange flower water, select raw cane sugar, which has a less pronounced taste. To skip the sugar altogether, a small amount of fruit will be sufficient to bring a little sweetness to a brioche batter, as will the addition of raisins. A more indulgent option is to incorporate some chocolate chips into the batter. For a panettone type version, add some bits of candied fruit or simply some raisins and some finely cut orange peel.

Raisin Brioche >

This batter, made chiefly of rice flour, has a shortbread texture. Flavored with orange flower water, it's a brioche that will be good for dessert as well as breakfast. Since it's a little sweet, you can enjoy it in slices with some honey or marmalade.

■ Cream together the margarine and sugar in a bowl. Add the eggs, one at a time.

■ Combine half the rice flour and all of the baking powder in a separate bowl. Add the rice milk and orange flower water and mix. Stir in the remainder of the rice flour and the raisins.

■ Pour the batter into an oiled bread pan or 4 small individual pans and bake at 375 degrees Fahrenheit for 20 minutes. Raise the heat to 400 degrees Fahrenheit and bake for an additional 15 minutes.

¾ cup vegetable margarine, softened

⅓ cup raw cane sugar

2 eggs

1½ cups rice flour

2 teaspoons baking powder

⅔ cup rice milk

⅓ cup orange flower water

⅓ cup raisins

Lemon Brioche >

For this brioche I chose to combine millet semolina with rice flour. This semolina, which looks like an extremely fine powder, lightens the batter. With little sugar, this brioche has a light and airy crumb that is good for snacks and breakfast.

- Combine the millet semolina, olive oil, and sugar in a bowl. Add the eggs, one at a time. Stir in the rice flour and baking powder. Then stir in the lemon zest.

- Pour into an oiled bread pan and bake at 400 degrees Fahrenheit for 35 minutes. Remove from the pan and let cool.

⅓ cup fine millet semolina

¼ cup olive oil

2½ tablespoons organic dark brown sugar or raw cane sugar

3 eggs

½ cup rice flour

1 teaspoon baking powder

Zest of 1 lemon, finely grated

Fruit Brioche

For this brioche I use a rice semolina, which has an extremely fine texture. The flavor of the olive oil is very unobtrusive, and the resulting consistency is similar to a cake, which makes it suitable for cutting into slices. It's sugar-free—only the fruit provides sweetness—so you might want to spread a bit of preserves on it.

- Pour the olive oil into a bowl and mix in the rice semolina and the eggs. Add the rice flour and baking powder and mix well. Stir in the essential oil and the pear.

- Pour into an oiled bread pan and bake at 400–425 degrees Fahrenheit for 35 minutes. Remove from the pan and let cool.

Banana Brioche: Omit the pear and essential oil and add 1 banana, sliced, and 1 pinch ground cinnamon.

¼ cup light olive oil

⅓ cup fine rice semolina

3 eggs

½ cup rice flour

1 teaspoon baking powder

6 drops grapefruit essential oil

1 pear, thinly sliced

Vanilla Quinoa Brioche

This batter turns out quite delicate. The flavor of the quinoa is subtle, while the vanilla dominates. Sliced for breakfast or snacks, it goes well with all types of marmalades and spreads.

■ Combine the eggs, sugar, and yogurt in a bowl. Pour in the olive oil, stirring vigorously. Mix in the rice flour, quinoa flour, baking powder, and powdered vanilla.

■ Pour into a bread pan coated with oil or vegetable margarine and bake at 425 degrees Fahrenheit for 15 minutes. Reduce the heat to 400 degrees Fahrenheit and bake for 15 minutes longer.

3 eggs

½ cup raw cane sugar or organic dark brown sugar

6 ounces (¾ cup) soy yogurt

¼ cup light olive oil

¾ cup rice flour

7 tablespoons quinoa flour

4 teaspoons baking powder

½ teaspoon powdered vanilla

Cakes

Making cakes ...

Which flours should you use in cake batters?

Rice flour can be used successfully in all types of cakes: génoises (sponge cakes), fruit cakes, pound cakes, and chocolate cakes. It can be used alone, but when it is mixed with other ingredients (such as very finely ground almonds, for example, or a fine rice semolina), you can obtain different and delicious textures.

Because of their rather strong flavors, I use quinoa and chestnut flours to complement rice flour. Add them in a smaller proportion or combine them with another strongly flavored ingredient like finely ground hazelnuts or cocoa. Chestnut flour blends well with either finely ground or puréed almonds or hazelnuts, chocolate, apples, or pears.

How to make a gluten-free cake rise

To obtain a tender and moist crumb, you will need to use a gluten-free baking powder (see page 11), or you can add stiffly beaten egg whites. With stiffly beaten egg whites in a batter, the amount of flour used will be minimal, as with Tropical Sponge Cake (page 36) and Ginger Cocoa Cake (page 52), or even none at all, as with Rich Chocolate Fondant Cake (page 46). The consistency of the batter should be semi-liquid. When a basic batter is very thick, you should choose baking powder instead.

... without gluten

Characteristics of gluten-free cake batters

To ensure that the batter rises properly, do not make very thick cakes and use either a layer cake pan or even a pie pan. This way your gluten-free cakes will be tender and moist; they will also offer the advantage of baking very quickly.

I use bread pans when I want to obtain a cake with a pound-cake-like texture, as with Chocolate Chip Pistachio Cake (page 44) and Almond Cake à l'Orange (page 38). Although the cakes may be slightly more delicate, these recipes are completely adapted to baking in a bread pan and provide a very delicious result when they are cut in large slices. You may sometimes need to protect the top of the cakes from high temperatures while the semi-liquid batter expands and bakes uniformly.

What kind of fat should you use?

Certain types of cakes, such as sponge cakes (génoises), don't need any fat at all. For other types, I like to use almond or hazelnut purées, which become vegetable "butters" that lend an absolutely extraordinary flavor. This generally produces cakes where the flavor of the oil-producing nuts is dominant.

To achieve batters that allow the flavors of the other ingredients to dominate, use a non-hydrogenated organic vegetable margarine. This creates a base that's easy to mix with sugar to make a wonderfully creamy batter.

In some of my recipes I use a light olive oil. See page 27 for some hints on delicately flavoring it.

Tropical Sponge Cake with Whipped Coconut Cream >

This batter results in a light sponge cake (génoise), thanks to confectioners' sugar and rice flour. The whipped cream is very quick to melt, but it will keep for several hours in the refrigerator. It is combined here with lychees, but it is equally tasty in fresh fruit tarts and in chocolate, banana, or coconut cakes!

■ To make the cake, place $1/2$ cup of the confectioners' sugar into a bowl, add the egg yolks, and beat well. Fold in the shredded coconut and rice flour. Beat the egg whites until stiff, and gently fold them into the batter.

■ Pour the batter about $1/2$ inch thick into a jelly-roll pan, rectangular cake pan, or 2 square cake pans lined with parchment paper. Bake at 425 degrees Fahrenheit for 15 to 20 minutes. The cake should be very lightly browned. Remove from the pan and let cool.

■ To make the whipped cream, beat the coconut cream and coconut oil with a whisk for several seconds to blend and smooth them out. Place in the refrigerator for 30 minutes, then beat with an electric mixer while adding the remaining $1/4$ cup confectioners' sugar, one tablespoon at a time. Beat 1 to 2 minutes, or until the cream has thickened a little. Keep the mixture refrigerated until you are ready to assemble the cake.

■ To assemble the cake, drain the canned lychees. If you baked the cake in one large pan, cut it in two so you have two cakes to stack. Place the first cake on a serving plate, spread it with the whipped coconut cream, arrange the lychees on top, stack the second cake layer on top of that, spread it with a thin coating of the whipped cream, and sprinkle with shredded coconut. Decorate with sliced rounds of kiwifruit and sliced mango or star fruit.

Note: Don't confuse coconut cream with the sweetened product used for making drinks. To get coconut cream, place a can of full-fat coconut milk in the refrigerator for at least two hours. Take care to keep the can upright, and do not shake it while opening. Scoop the solid cream off the top (about one-third to one-half of the can will turn into solid cream).

$3/4$ cup confectioners' sugar

4 eggs, separated

$1/2$ cup unsweetened shredded dried coconut, plus more for decoration

$1/4$ cup rice flour

$1/2$ cup coconut cream (see note)

$1/4$ cup coconut oil

1 (20-ounce) can lychees in syrup

1 kiwifruit, for decoration

1 mango or star fruit, for decoration

Almond Cake à l'Orange   >

A fragrant cake, delicious with tea.

■ Melt the margarine in a medium saucepan over low heat. Remove from the heat and stir in the sugar, finely ground almonds, and vanilla extract. Mix in the eggs, one at a time. Then mix in the rice flour, baking powder, and orange zest.

■ Pour into an oiled bread pan and bake at 400 degrees Fahrenheit for 10 minutes. Raise the heat to 425 degrees Fahrenheit and bake for 15 to 20 minutes longer. This cake batter tends to brown very quickly, so you may need to protect it during baking.

⅓ cup vegetable margarine

½ cup raw cane sugar

½ cup finely ground blanched almonds

6 drops vanilla extract

3 eggs

¾ cup rice flour

1 teaspoon baking powder

1 tablespoon orange zest

Chocolate Cake Impérial

This is a very moist chocolate cake that can be served warm for dessert accompanied by an almond sauce, English cream, or bitter orange marmalade. It's best to use a dark baking chocolate that's a minimum of 60% cocoa.

■ Melt the chocolate and margarine in a medium saucepan over very low heat. Remove from the heat and add the sugar and quinoa flour. Add the egg yolks, one at a time. Beat the egg whites until stiff and gently fold them into the chocolate batter.

■ Pour into a heavily oiled cake pan and bake at 400–425 degrees Fahrenheit for 25 minutes.

7 ounces dark baking chocolate

7 tablespoons vegetable margarine

⅓ cup organic dark brown sugar

2½ tablespoons quinoa flour

4 eggs, separated

<
Cinnamon Marble Cake

⅓ cup vegetable margarine, softened

½ cup raw cane sugar

⅓ cup finely ground blanched almonds

3 eggs

¾ cup rice flour

1 teaspoon baking powder

1 tablespoon ground cinnamon

A very flavorful cake, it goes well with compotes or fruit salads. If you are especially fond of cinnamon, you can double the amount to make the flavor more intense. Enjoy this cake with afternoon tea or for breakfast.

■ Cream the margarine with the sugar. Add the finely ground almonds and the eggs, one at a time. Stir in the rice flour and baking powder.

■ Mix well. Pour half of the batter into an oiled cake pan. Add the cinnamon to the remaining batter and drop it by spoonfuls into the pan on top of the other batter. Draw a knife through the batter in an irregular pattern to make swirls.

■ Bake at 400–425 degrees Fahrenheit for 25 to 30 minutes. The cake is done when a knife blade inserted in the center comes out dry.

Pear Cake with Hazelnuts

⅓ cup hazelnuts

3 eggs, separated

⅓ cup organic dark brown sugar

3 tablespoons rice flour

1 teaspoon baking powder

2 pears, peeled and sliced

3 to 4 tablespoons chopped hazelnuts

Hazelnut purée, which takes the place of margarine, gives a unique flavor to this cake. It is made delicate by the addition of stiffly whipped egg whites.

■ To make a hazelnut purée, place the hazelnuts in a saucepan and cover with water. Bring to a boil, lower the heat, and simmer for 30 minutes. Do not drain (keeping them moist will help the skins come off more easily and prevent the nuts from drying out). Let cool just until the nuts can be easily handled. While the nuts are still warm, remove as much of the brown skin as possible. Drain lightly, transfer to a food processor, and purée until smooth.

■ Pour the hazelnut purée into a bowl, add the egg yolks, and mix well. Stir in the sugar. Whip the egg whites until stiff and fold half of them into the batter, mixing well. Add the flour and baking powder, then fold in the remaining egg whites.

■ Pour the batter into an oiled cake pan and arrange the pear slices around the top. They will sink into the cake. Bake at 425 degrees Fahrenheit for 30 minutes. Remove from the pan and sprinkle with the chopped hazelnuts to decorate.

Round Apple Cake with Fruit Syrup and Creamy Almond Butter >

This cake is baked in a tart pan. You can enjoy it while still warm, accompanied by Creamy Almond Butter.

7 tablespoons vegetable margarine, softened

1/3 cup apple juice concentrate

3 eggs

2/3 cup rice flour

2 apples, peeled and thinly sliced

Ground cinnamon

Creamy Almond Butter (below; optional)

■ Place the margarine in a bowl and add the juice concentrate. Mix well. Add 1 of the eggs and the rice flour and mix well. Then add the remaining 2 eggs.

■ Pour into an oiled tart pan and arrange the apples around the top so the slices overlap. Bake at 400 degrees Fahrenheit for 30 minutes. Remove from the oven and dust with cinnamon. Serve with Creamy Almond Butter, if desired.

Creamy Almond Butter

A very fast and extremely easy way to make a cream that truly melts in your mouth. Its texture resembles a butter cream.

6 ounces (3/4 cup) soy yogurt

3 tablespoons almond butter

1 1/2 tablespoons agave syrup

■ Pour the soy yogurt into a bowl, add the almond butter, and stir vigorously. Stir in the agave syrup.

■ Place in the refrigerator for 30 minutes so the cream congeals slightly. Serve in a bowl so everyone can put a dollop on their own piece of cake.

Almond Cream

Use this topping for Hazelnut Cake, page 44.

3/4 cup blanched almonds

3/4 cup water

2 tablespoons confectioners' sugar

■ Combine the almonds and water in a blender and process on high speed for several minutes until smooth. Stop occasionally to scrape down the sides of the blender jar, if necessary. Add the confectioners' sugar and continue to blend until completely smooth. Pour into a sauce boat and serve on the side.

Chocolate Chip Pistachio Cake >

Bits of pear, pistachio, and creamy chocolate are found at the heart of this moist and indulgent cake. You can also bake the batter in paper-lined muffin pans for take-along snacks or a petits-fours-style presentation.

■ Melt the margarine in a saucepan over very low heat. Remove from the heat and stir in ½ cup of the sugar. Add the rice flour and eggs, one at a time.

■ Add the diced pear, 20 pistachios, and chocolate chips to the batter. Pour into an oiled cake pan or muffin tin lined with paper muffin cups and bake at 425 degrees Fahrenheit for 25 to 35 minutes. Remove from the pan and let cool.

■ Grind the 2 tablespoons pistachios for decoration in a blender or food processor. Add the remaining 2 tablespoons sugar to the ground pistachios and sprinkle over the cake.

7 tablespoons vegetable margarine

½ cup plus 2 tablespoons raw cane sugar

⅔ cup rice flour

3 eggs

1 pear or apple, peeled, quartered, and diced

About 20 shelled unsalted pistachios, plus 2 table-spoons or more for decoration

2 tablespoons chocolate chips

Hazelnut Cake with Almond Cream

Thanks to hazelnut purée, which takes the place of margarine, this cake batter made with rice flour has a moist and tender crumb. You can also double the amounts and make two cakes to layer with filling and a ganache.

■ To make a hazelnut purée, place the hazelnuts in a saucepan and cover with water. Bring to a boil, lower the heat, and simmer for 30 minutes. Do not drain (keeping them moist will help the skins come off more easily and prevent the nuts from drying out). Let cool just until the nuts can be easily handled. While the nuts are still warm, remove as much of the brown skin as possible. Drain lightly, transfer to a food processor, and purée until smooth.

■ To make the cake, transfer the hazelnut purée to a bowl, add the sugar, and mix vigorously until very smooth. Beat in the egg yolks, one at a time. Stir in the rice flour and mix well. Whip the egg whites and fold them into the batter. Pour into an 8-inch round cake pan and bake at 400 degrees Fahrenheit for 20 minutes. Cool completely and top with Almond Cream.

⅓ cup hazelnuts

⅓ cup raw cane sugar

3 eggs, separated

⅓ cup rice flour

Almond Cream, page 42

Orange Caramel Cake >

As a variation, replace the orange slices with pineapple bits or mango slices, and use grapefruit essential oil instead of mandarin or tangerine.

■ Coat the bottom of a cake pan with a little margarine and arrange the orange slices over it. Dust the orange slices with ¼ cup of the sugar.

■ Cream together the 7 tablespoons margarine and remaining ½ cup sugar in a bowl. Add 1 of the eggs and mix well. Mix in the rice flour. Then add the remaining 2 eggs. Mix vigorously while adding the drops of essential oil.

■ Pour the batter over the orange slices in the cake pan. It might seem that there isn't enough batter, but it will spread out as it bakes and fill in the bare spots.

■ Bake at 400 degrees Fahrenheit for 20 minutes. Remove from the pan while still warm, as the caramel oranges may stick to the pan as they cool. The cake should be inverted so the orange slices are on top. The cake can be cut into individual shapes with a knife or cookie cutter for a more elaborate presentation.

1 orange, peeled and thinly sliced

¾ cup raw cane sugar

7 tablespoons vegetable margarine, softened

3 eggs

⅔ cup rice flour

4 drops mandarin or tangerine essential oil

Rich Chocolate Fondant Cake

This is a flourless cake that is best enjoyed after it has cooled. Rich in chocolate, you will discern the subtle bits of chestnut as you eat it.

■ Combine the margarine, sugar, and chocolate in a saucepan and melt over low heat. Remove from the heat and let cool. Add the egg yolks, one at a time, beating vigorously after each addition. Stir in the vanilla extract.

■ Add the chestnuts, crushing them coarsely with the back of a wooden spoon while mixing them in. Whip the egg whites into peaks and fold them gently into the batter.

■ Pour into a layer cake pan and bake at 400-425 degrees Fahrenheit for 25 minutes. Cool the cake completely before serving. Top with the slivered almonds and dust with cocoa powder. Keep in a cool place but do not refrigerate in order to keep its chewy texture.

Note: The cake can be served directly from the pan. If you prefer to remove it from the pan, line the pan with parchment paper before baking, and let the cake cool completely before removing it.

⅔ cup vegetable margarine

½ cup organic dark brown sugar

3.5 ounces dark baking chocolate (70% cocoa)

4 eggs, separated

1 teaspoon vanilla extract

1½ cups roasted chestnuts

3 tablespoons slivered almonds

Unsweetened cocoa powder

< Dried Fruit Rolls

3/4 cup whole almonds

3 dried figs (see note), stems removed

1 piece candied orange peel

1/2 teaspoon grated orange zest

3 tablespoons rice syrup

4 rice paper rounds (8 to 9 inches in diameter)

3 tablespoons coarsely chopped walnuts

Ground cinnamon

Note: When purchasing the dried figs, make sure they are not dusted with flour.

Made with rice sheets, these crispy rolls hide a filling of dried fruits flavored with candied orange peel. A fanciful version of Galette des rois (pastry traditionally eaten on Twelfth Night in France, containing a charm), the lucky token can be slipped into one of the rolls.

■ Place the almonds, figs, candied orange peel, and orange zest in a food processor with the S blade and process until finely ground. Add the rice syrup and process until evenly incorporated.

■ Place each rice sheet on a dish towel that has been dampened with water, or soak the rice sheets very briefly in water, just until softened. Spread 2 tablespoons of the almond mixture in a horizontal line on the upper part of each rice sheet. Sprinkle with some of the walnuts. Fold in the left and right sides of the rice sheet over the filling, then roll like a flute.

■ Heat a small amount of oil in a skillet and brown the fruit rolls, one or two at a time. Drain on paper towels and dust with cinnamon.

Bergamot-Flavored Apple Pound Cake

7 tablespoons vegetable margarine, softened

1/2 cup raw cane sugar

4 drops bergamot essential oil

3 eggs

2/3 cup rice flour

1 teaspoon baking powder

2 apples, peeled and diced

To obtain a moist and light cake when using rice flour, start with a very warm oven so the cake will expand. Then reduce the temperature later so the center of the cake can bake without scorching the exterior.

■ Preheat the oven to 425 degrees Fahrenheit. Place the margarine and sugar in a bowl and stir until well combined. Add the essential oil and the eggs, one at a time, mixing well after each addition. Then mix in the flour and baking powder. Stir in the apples.

■ Pour into a lightly oiled bread pan and bake for 20 minutes. Lower the temperature to 400 degrees Fahrenheit and bake for 20 minutes longer.

My Baba
with Lemon Syrup >

This is a melt-in-your-mouth dessert. The batter, which contains a little potato starch (look for organic), has a texture that perfectly soaks up the lemon-flavored agave syrup.

3 lemons

1/3 cup rice flour

1/3 cup raw cane sugar

5 tablespoons potato starch

4 teaspoons baking powder

3 eggs

2 tablespoons olive oil

4 tablespoons plus
1 teaspoon agave syrup

■ Using a vegetable peeler, remove 3 small bands of lemon peel from the lemons. Cut the peel into fine strips with scissors and set it aside.

■ Combine the rice flour, sugar, potato starch, and baking powder in a bowl. Make a well, crack the eggs, and add them along with the olive oil. Mix the batter vigorously—it should be light and foamy. Stir in the reserved lemon peel.

■ Pour into an oiled baba au rhum pan (baba mold) and bake at 400 degrees Fahrenheit for 20 to 30 minutes. Take care to check the cake, as the batter browns easily.

■ While the cake is baking, make the lemon syrup. Squeeze the lemons to obtain 3/4 to 1 cup juice. Pour the juice into a small saucepan and warm it briefly over low heat. Add the agave syrup. Remove from the heat and immediately pour over the warm cake (still in the pan) so the syrup can soak in. Let cool.

Note: If the lemon juice is a little sour, reduce the amount of juice and dilute it with a little water or a little more agave syrup.

Yogurt Cake >

Easy and quick to prepare, this is a practical cake to take along on an outing. It can be made plain, without adding the apples. If you choose a fruit-flavored yogurt (peach, cherry, or strawberry, for example), it will impart a subtle flavor. If you choose a plain yogurt, flavor it with lemon zest, a few drops of orange essential oil, or a spoonful of ground cinnamon.

■ Combine the yogurt and rice syrup in a bowl. Add the olive oil, then add the semolina. Stir well while adding the rice flour, baking powder, and eggs. Fold the optional apples into the batter.

■ Pour into an oiled cake pan and bake at 425 degrees Fahrenheit for 20 to 30 minutes.

6 ounces (¾ cup) soy yogurt, plain or with fruit

⅔ cup rice syrup or honey

½ cup olive oil

⅓ cup fine rice or millet semolina, or additional rice flour

1⅓ cups rice flour

4 teaspoons baking powder

2 eggs

2 apples, peeled and thinly sliced (optional)

Ginger Cocoa Cake

Light and airy, this cake is made with dark chocolate and a hint of ginger, then topped with finely sliced pears.

■ Combine the chocolate, rice milk, and optional sugar in a saucepan, and warm over low heat until the chocolate is melted. Remove from the heat and stir in the olive oil. Mix well. Cool slightly; then add the egg yolks, one at a time. Mix in the rice flour and ginger.

■ Beat the egg whites into stiff peaks and fold them gently into the batter. Pour into an oiled cake pan (or line the pan with parchment paper), and arrange the pear slices on top. Bake at 400–425 degrees Fahrenheit for 30 minutes.

■ This cake is cut right in the pan. If you wish to remove it from the pan, line the pan with parchment paper before pouring in the batter.

Note: Instead of mincing the ginger slice, you can place it in a garlic press and crush it before adding it to the batter.

3.5 ounces dark baking chocolate (70% cocoa)

½ cup rice milk or soymilk

2 to 3 tablespoons organic dark brown sugar (for a sweeter cake; optional)

¼ cup light olive oil

4 eggs, separated

¼ cup rice flour

1 thin slice fresh ginger, very finely minced

2 ripe pears, peeled and sliced

< Amaranth Snow-Topped Cake

Appreciated at teas and birthday parties, this cake, coated with a chocolate ganache, is covered with tiny white grains of puffed amaranth. If you choose to use organic dark brown sugar, the sweetness of the cake will be more full-bodied than if you choose raw organic sugar.

Cake

1/3 cup hazelnuts

3 eggs, separated

1/2 cup raw organic sugar or organic dark brown sugar

7 tablespoons rice milk

1 2/3 cups chestnut flour

1/4 cup cocoa powder

1 teaspoon baking powder

1 1/2 to 1 3/4 cups plain puffed amaranth or puffed quinoa

■ To make the cake, first make a hazelnut purée. Place the hazelnuts in a saucepan and cover with water. Bring to a boil, lower the heat, and simmer for 30 minutes. Do not drain (keeping them moist will help the skins come off more easily and prevent the nuts from drying out). Let cool just until the nuts can be easily handled. While the nuts are still warm, remove as much of the brown skin as possible. Drain lightly, transfer to a food processor, and purée until smooth.

■ Transfer the hazelnut purée to a bowl and add the egg yolks and sugar. While stirring, add the rice milk, chestnut flour, cocoa powder, and baking powder. Beat the egg whites into stiff peaks and fold them into the batter. Pour into a cake pan and bake at 425 degrees Fahrenheit for 20 minutes.

Chocolate Ganache

7 ounces dark chocolate (more than 70% cocoa)

1/3 cup rice milk or water

1 cup soy cream

Vanilla seeds, or 4 drops orange essential oil (optional)

■ To make the chocolate ganache, combine the chocolate and rice milk in a small saucepan and place over very low heat until the chocolate melts. Add several spoonfuls of the soy cream, stirring constantly. Continue to mix in the soy cream, a little at a time, stirring constantly. Occasionally lift the pan from the heat and then replace it (in order to keep the mixture warm and the consistency creamy). Add the optional vanilla seeds and mix well.

■ Immediately spread the ganache over the cake with a spatula or the back of a spoon. Sprinkle the puffed amaranth over the ganache. Let cool.

Making pastry crusts ... without gluten

Mixing and Spreading

■ Unlike wheat flour, rice, quinoa, and chestnut flours cannot simply be combined with water and a small amount of some type of fat to make a supple pastry crust. Nor is a gluten-free pastry crust as easy to form.

■ But to make a pie or tart it isn't absolutely necessary to make a crust that's rolled. You can just as well use a cake batter and pour it into a large tart pan or pie dish that isn't very deep. After baking, you'll have a "crust" ready to garnish. It's a solution I find very easy and delicious for all toppings with cream and fresh fruits, such as raspberries or kiwifruit rounds.

■ For these fresh fruit tarts, prepare a génoise (sponge cake) style batter, or even a yogurt cake batter, and pour it into a large pan lined with parchment paper. The batter should be about one-third inch thick. You can even use a batter for madeleines or biscuits, which creates a tart base that's both original and tasty. Bake and let cool. Then spread it with a cream (such as Vanilla Pastry Cream, page 126, or a thick, sweet-flavored soy cream) and garnish with fruits of your choice.

■ For chocolate or chestnut cream tarts, use cake recipes to make the base of the tart that contain a rich, high-fat purée. The result will be very tasty.

■ If you need a base with a rim for a more traditional tart or pie, you can make a dough with rice flour or quinoa flour, as in the recipe for Apricot Tart with Almond Crumb Topping (page 69). Keep in mind, however, that it will not have the same elasticity as a dough with a wheat base. You will need to spread it directly in the pan by pushing the dough with your fingers or rolling it out on a plastic-covered placemat to spread the dough a little more easily.

■ To obtain a crispy dough, I have used finely ground almonds (see the recipe for Creamy Apple Pie, page 59).

Tarts

< Creamy Apple Pie

The crust for this pie is crispy, thanks to the combination of rice flour and finely ground almonds. Beneath the fondant of fruits, the soy cream makes a creamy filling flavored with cinnamon.

■ To make the crust, knead together the margarine, sugar, and almonds in a bowl. Add the eggs and as much rice flour as necessary to form a ball of dough. In order to roll it out easily, place some plastic wrap over the ball of dough and roll it out directly onto a piece of parchment paper. Line a pie pan with the pastry dough.

■ To make the filling, combine the soy cream with the sugar, cinnamon, almonds, candied orange peel, and raisins. Spread over the pastry dough in the pie pan. Arrange the sliced apples on top, overlapping them. Bake at 400 degrees Fahrenheit for 30 to 40 minutes.

Strawberry Tart over Almond Biscuit >>

A cake batter baked in a large tart pan provides a base for you to spread a pastry cream (or a dessert cream made with soymilk or rice milk and flavored with vanilla) before arranging the strawberries on top.

■ To make the almond biscuit, knead the margarine with the sugar in a bowl. Add the finely ground almonds. Then add the eggs, one at a time. Stir in the rice flour and baking powder. Mix well and spread into a large tart pan or pie pan. Bake at 400 degrees Fahrenheit for 10 minutes. Raise the temperature to 425 degrees Fahrenheit and continue baking for 15 minutes longer. (As this cake batter tends to brown very quickly, you may need to protect it during baking.)

■ To make the pastry cream, combine the egg yolks and sugar in a small saucepan. Add the rice flour and stir in the soymilk. Place over low heat, stirring constantly, until the mixture begins to thicken. Remove from the heat and flavor with the optional rose water.

■ To assemble, remove the almond biscuit from the pan and spread it with the warm cream. Let cool so it sets. If the berries are small, arrange them whole over the cream; if they are large, cut them in half. Serve at once.

Raspberry Tart over Almond Biscuit: Replace the strawberries with an equal amount of fresh raspberries.

Strawberry Tart
over Almond Biscuit

Orange Tart >

A delicious hint of orange zest is found in the filling and the shortbread crust. The crust is also ideal for cheesecake fillings and flans. For a lemon version of the crust, just replace the orange peel with lemon peel.

■ To make the crust, combine the rice flour, eggs, sugar, almonds, margarine, and orange zest in a food processor. Mix the dough well until it forms a ball. If necessary, add a bit more flour. The dough should be easy to knead but not necessarily easy to roll out.

■ Spread the dough directly in a tart pan by flattening it with your fingers (this is especially easy for little tartlet pans). Alternatively, put a bit of plastic wrap over the ball of dough and flatten it with a rolling pin directly onto a piece of parchment paper. Then line a tart pan with the dough.

■ To make the filling, remove some of the orange peel with a vegetable peeler to obtain a piece about as large as two orange sections. Juice the oranges and place the juice, peel, eggs, sugar, and cream of rice in a blender. Process until smooth and well blended. Pour into the prepared crust and bake at 425 degrees Fahrenheit for 30 to 35 minutes.

Shortbread Crust

1 1/2 cups rice flour, more or less as needed

2 eggs

1/3 cup raw cane sugar

1/3 cup finely ground blanched almonds

1/4 cup vegetable margarine, softened

1/3 to 1 teaspoon grated orange zest

Orange Filling

2 oranges

2 eggs

4 tablespoons raw cane sugar

2 tablespoons cream of rice (farina)

< Chestnut Cream Tart

1/2 cup ground blanched almonds

1/3 cup raw cane sugar

3 eggs

1/3 cup chestnut flour (sift, if lumpy)

1.75 ounces dark chocolate (70% cocoa)

2/3 cup Almond and Chestnut Cream (page 114)

Several squares of chocolate for chocolate shavings (optional)

A delicate cake batter made with chestnut flour and baked in a tart pan makes an excellent base for an indulgent garnish: chocolate is spread as a glaze under the chestnut cream.

■ Combine the ground almonds and sugar in a bowl. Add the eggs and mix well. Add the chestnut flour and mix until thoroughly combined.

■ Pour into an 8-inch tart pan or cake pan that has been lined with parchment paper. Bake at 400 degrees Fahrenheit for 20 minutes. Remove from the oven and place the dark chocolate on top of the tart. When the chocolate has melted, spread it using a spatula to coat the surface of the cake. Let cool. When the chocolate has firmed up, spread a layer of Almond and Chestnut Cream over it. Decorate with chocolate shavings, if desired.

Nougatine Tartlets >

*A hazelnut cake batter serves here as a base for creating
dainty chocolate tartlets. Ungarnished,
they also make delicious small cookies.*

■ To make the nougatine, chop 1 cup of the hazelnuts in a
food processor and transfer to a bowl.

■ To make a hazelnut purée, place the remaining $\frac{1}{4}$ cup
hazelnuts in a saucepan and cover with water. Bring to a boil,
lower the heat, and simmer for 30 minutes. Do not drain
(keeping them moist will help the skins come off more easily
and prevent the nuts from drying out). Let cool just until the
nuts can be easily handled. While the nuts are still warm,
remove as much of the brown skin as possible. Drain lightly,
transfer to a food processor, and purée until smooth.

■ Add the hazelnut purée to the chopped hazelnuts in the
bowl. Stir in the confectioners' sugar, chestnut flour, and rice
milk. This will make a thick batter. Scoop the batter onto a
baking sheet lined with parchment paper, and shape it into a
small log. With the blade of a knife, flatten it to a thickness
of about $\frac{1}{2}$ inch to obtain a long, almost rectangular shape.
Bake at 425 degrees Fahrenheit for 20 minutes. Remove from
the oven and cut into several small squares. Let cool.

■ To make the ganache, break the chocolate into several
pieces and place it in a saucepan with the rice milk and sugar.
Place over low heat until the chocolate melts. Remove from
the heat and add the soy cream and mandarin essential oil.
Stir vigorously or use an electric beater to obtain a very
smooth cream. Place in the refrigerator for at least 1 hour.
The cream will thicken as it cools.

■ Cut the candied orange peel into fine, bezeled slices or
small triangles. Using a small spoon, place a spoonful of the
cream ganache on each piece of the nougatine, forming it
into a small dome. Alternate the final decoration, placing a
whole hazelnut on some pieces and a piece of candied
orange peel on others. Lay them out on a tray like checkers
on a checkerboard.

Nougatine

1 $\frac{1}{4}$ cups whole hazelnuts,
plus a few more for
decoration

$\frac{1}{2}$ cup confectioners' sugar

$\frac{1}{3}$ cup chestnut flour

3 tablespoons rice milk

Cream Ganache

3.5 ounces dark chocolate

$\frac{1}{4}$ cup rice milk

2 tablespoons raw cane
sugar

1 cup thick soy cream

2 drops mandarin
essential oil

1 piece candied orange peel

< Apricot Tart with Almond Crumb Topping

Almond Crumb Topping

1 1/2 cups finely ground almonds

1/2 cup organic dark brown sugar

1 teaspoon ground cinnamon

Apricot Tart

1 cup rice flour

1/2 cup plus 1 tablespoon quinoa flour

4 tablespoons rice syrup or honey

2 tablespoons olive oil

Several spoonfuls soymilk, rice milk, or almond milk

12 apricots

The batter for this tart is lightly sweetened with rice syrup, and the finely ground almond crumb topping lends sweetness to the apricots.

■ To make the crumb topping, combine the almonds, sugar, and cinnamon in a bowl. Set aside.

■ To make the tart, blend the rice flour, quinoa flour, rice syrup, and olive oil in a food processor. Add a few spoonfuls of soymilk, as needed, in order to obtain a well-blended ball of dough. Flour a countertop and rolling pin and roll out the pastry. Transfer it to a tart pan or pie pan.

■ Pit the apricots and cut them into quarters. Arrange them skin side down in the bottom of the pastry shell. Bake at 425 degrees Fahrenheit for 15 minutes.

■ Sprinkle the crumb topping over the hot fruit and return the tart to the oven for 15 minutes longer. Check to be sure the topping does not get too brown.

< Kiwifruit Tartlets

Rich cream and bits of vanilla bean and coconut flakes make these tartlets a festive dessert.

Tartlet Crust

$1/3$ cup coconut cream (see note), at room temperature

$1/3$ cup organic dark brown sugar, packed

$1\,1/4$ cups rice flour

■ To make the tartlet crust, whisk or blend the coconut cream until it is smooth. Add the sugar and stir until blended. Stir in the rice flour to make a thick dough that is firm enough to roll into a ball. Divide the dough into 5 or 6 pieces and put them into 5 or 6 tartlet pans. Press the dough with your fingers to spread it evenly without making a rim (it will be too sticky to roll out with a rolling pin). Bake at 400–425 degrees Fahrenheit for about 20 minutes. Cool completely and remove from the pans.

Vanilla Cream

$1/3$ cup rice flour

1 cup rice milk

2 tablespoons raw cane sugar

$1/2$ vanilla bean

■ To make the vanilla cream, combine the rice flour and rice milk in a small saucepan. Place over low heat and stir continuously until thickened. Add the sugar and stir until it is melted and the cream is quite thick. Remove from the heat. Split the vanilla bean pod in half and remove the seeds with the tip of a knife. Add the seeds to the cream.

Fruit Topping

3 or 4 kiwifruits

Tropical fruits of your choice (mango, pineapple, papaya, or banana; optional)

3 tablespoons unsweetened shredded coconut

■ Spread the warm cream on the bottom of the tartlet crusts. Just before serving, peel and thinly slice the kiwifruits and other fruit of your choice, if using. Arrange the slices on top of the cream. Sprinkle with the shredded coconut, and serve.

Note: Don't confuse coconut cream with the sweetened product used for making drinks. To get coconut cream, place a can of full-fat coconut milk in the refrigerator for at least two hours. Take care to keep the can upright, and do not shake it while opening. Scoop the solid cream off the top (about one-third to one-half of the can will turn into solid cream).

Blueberry Tart

A great pleasure to eat! In this moist batter, the juice of the blueberries soaks into the cream, which is added toward the end of baking. If you don't have fresh blueberries, you can prepare this dessert with canned blueberries.

■ To make the tart crust, combine the sugar and margarine in a bowl. Add the lemon zest and eggs, one at a time. Then stir in the flour and baking powder. Pour the batter into a cake pan lined with parchment paper, and bake at 400 degrees Fahrenheit for 20 minutes.

■ To make the topping, combine the egg, soy cream, and sugar in a bowl. As soon as the cake begins to brown (after about 20 minutes of baking), spread the topping from the center to the edges. Sprinkle the blueberries on top and return to the oven for 10 minutes longer. Let cool completely before removing from the pan.

Tart Crust

½ cup raw cane sugar

7 tablespoons vegetable margarine, softened

Grated zest of 1 lemon

3 eggs

⅔ cup rice flour

1 teaspoon baking powder

Blueberry Topping

1 egg

3 large tablespoons thick soy cream

2 tablespoons raw cane sugar

1¼ cups fresh blueberries or drained canned blueberries

Pear and Candied Orange Delight

The base of this tart is very chewy, with an almond flavor that welcomes finely placed slices of pear. For a special touch, a layer of chocolate is added when it is removed from the oven.

■ Place the almonds in a food processor with a few tablespoons of water. Process into a smooth purée, adding a little more water as needed.

■ Vigorously mix the egg whites and sugar with the puréed almonds. Add the candied orange peel. Pour the batter into a small 8-inch tart pan lined with parchment paper. Arrange the pears on top like a rosette. Bake at 400 degrees Fahrenheit for 20 minutes.

■ Remove from the oven and scatter the chocolate over the surface of the cake. It will melt rapidly and glaze the pear slices. Let cool.

⅔ cup blanched almonds

4 egg whites

4 tablespoons raw cane sugar

2 tablespoons minced candied orange peel

2 pears, peeled and thinly sliced

4 to 6 squares chocolate, sliced or grated

Clafoutis

(Fruit Cobbler)

< Peach or Pear Clafoutis

⅔ cup finely ground
almonds

⅔ cup organic dark
brown sugar

⅔ cup rice flour

3 eggs

1 cup rice milk

3 pears or 4 peaches,
peeled and sliced

This batter, where the proportion of ground almonds and rice flour is equal, is perfectly suited for juicy fruits: apricots, peaches, or nectarines for a summer recipe; pears for an autumn clafoutis.

■ Preheat the oven to 400–425 degrees Fahrenheit, and oil a glass or earthenware cake pan or loaf pan.

■ Combine the almonds, sugar, and rice flour in a bowl. Add the eggs and mix while adding the rice milk, a little at a time. Fold the fruit into the batter. Pour into the prepared pan and bake for 30 minutes.

Chestnut Flour Clafoutis

4 apples, peeled and
thinly sliced

4 eggs

3 tablespoons organic dark
brown sugar

3⅓ cups sifted
chestnut flour

2 cups plus 2 tablespoons
soymilk, rice milk,
or almond milk

Chestnut flour contributes a sugary sweetness that complements the flavors of autumn. Quick to prepare, this dessert can be enriched with prunes or raisins.

■ Preheat the oven to 425–450 degrees Fahrenheit. Oil a cake pan and arrange the apples in it.

■ Beat together the eggs and sugar in a bowl. Add the chestnut flour, alternating with the soymilk. Pour over the apples and bake for 30 minutes.

Variation: If you prefer the flavor of the chestnut flour to be less prominent, replace half of it with rice flour.

Notes: Depending upon the quality of the chestnuts used, the flour might be either sweet and flavorful, or strong with a less-agreeable odor. It may sometimes be necessary to try several different flours before finding the one that will give the best results. Organic products often have the finest flavor, especially if they are fresh. Keep the chestnut flour in a cool place and use it quickly.

Ginger Pear Flan   >

The pear fondant is enhanced by a hint of ginger in this creamy, clafoutis-style dessert.

■ Preheat the oven to 425 degrees Fahrenheit. Combine the almonds, sugar, and rice flour in a bowl. Add the eggs, one at a time, and mix in the rice milk. Place the slice of ginger into a garlic press and crush it to obtain the juice and a little of the pulp. Stir it into the batter.

■ Fold the pears into the batter, and pour into a large, oiled glass baking pan or tart pan (about 12 inches in diameter). Bake immediately for 30 to 40 minutes. Let cool before eating.

3/4 cup chopped almonds

2/3 cup organic dark brown sugar

2/3 cup rice flour

3 eggs

2 cups rice milk, almond milk, or soymilk

1 slice fresh ginger

3 or 4 pears, peeled and thinly sliced

Banana and Coconut Milk Clafoutis

An exotically flavored dessert, this recipe uses canned coconut milk, which can be found in the organic section. Be sure to pre-heat the oven, because clafoutis batter with a rice flour base needs to be heated quickly so it inflates well and doesn't fall.

■ Preheat the oven to 400–425 degrees Fahrenheit. Pour the coconut milk into a saucepan and warm it just a bit so it's smooth.

■ Put the flour and sugar into a bowl, add the eggs, and stir in the coconut milk. Mix vigorously. Add the bananas to the batter. Pour immediately into a cake pan, and bake for 25 to 30 minutes.

1 2/3 cups coconut milk

1 cup rice flour

1/2 cup organic dark brown sugar

3 eggs

2 bananas, sliced into rounds

Apple Pistachio Clafoutis >

A particularly tasty dessert, especially while it's still warm.

■ Preheat the oven to 400–425 degrees Fahrenheit. Combine the rice flour, sugar, and almonds in a bowl. Add the eggs, one at a time, and the vanilla extract, if using. Mix in the rice milk, a little at a time, while stirring well.

■ Coarsely chop the pistachios with a knife or in a food processor. Add to the batter along with the apples and lemon zest.

■ Pour the batter into an oiled cake pan and bake immediately in the preheated oven (the clafoutis batter must be put immediately into the heat to inflate well without falling) for 20 to 30 minutes.

¾ cup rice flour

½ cup raw cane sugar

⅓ cup finely ground almonds

3 eggs

6 drops vanilla extract (optional)

¾ cup rice milk

2 handfuls (about 6 tablespoons) shelled unsalted pistachios

2 apples, peeled and thinly sliced

½ teaspoon lemon zest

Caramel Clafoutis

To give this clafoutis a caramel color, I use a fruit concentrate. The batter, which uses only natural sugar (fructose), has a slightly tart flavor. To sweeten it a bit more, you can add a handful of raisins.

■ Preheat the oven to 400–425 degrees Fahrenheit. Pour the juice concentrate into a bowl and mix in the eggs, one at a time. Add the rice flour, then add the rice milk. Fold the pears into the batter. Stir well.

■ Pour into a well-oiled cake pan. Bake immediately for 25 minutes.

¾ cup apple juice concentrate

3 eggs

1 cup rice flour

¾ cup rice milk

2 pears, peeled and sliced

Making crumbles and pudding ... without gluten

How do you make a crumble mixture?

Finely ground blanched almonds mixed with ground cinnamon and sugar make a quick and easy-to-prepare crumble that needs no additional fat since it already has the richness of almonds. This mixture absorbs the fruit juice, turns golden brown, and makes an absolutely delicious dessert. You can make variations with finely ground hazelnuts, grated coconut, or finely ground raw almonds.

For a crumble made with flour, choose chestnut. You can also make a crumble with buckwheat flour. Since its flavor is quite pronounced, however, mix it with something mild, such as finely ground hazelnuts.

Another solution is to use rice flakes mixed with margarine and sugar. This will produce a crustier crumble.

As for sugar, you can use raw cane or another type, depending on your taste, but why not try rice syrup as well?

Don't hesitate to enrich your crumble topping with raisins, dates, or dried apricots cut into small bits. These can replace sugar if you like things less sugary or if the fruit compote in your dish is very sweet.

What ingredients should you use to replace bread in your puddings?

Traditionally, a French pudding is made with leftover bread or bread crumbs. Replacing this basic ingredient with gluten-free flaked grains allows you to discover a lighter and more easily digested dessert. I have chosen to principally use rice flakes. You can add quinoa or millet flakes, but do so in small quantities since they have a very pronounced flavor.

You can even avoid adding eggs if you use bananas, which allow mixtures to gel somewhat after cooking.

Crumbles and Puddings

Fruit Pudding with Rice Flakes

1¾ cups rice flakes

1¼ cups rice milk

4 tablespoons coconut milk

4 dried pineapple rounds, diced

1 handful (about 3 tablespoons) raisins

⅓ cup organic dark brown sugar

2 eggs

2 bananas, or 1 banana and 1 apple, peeled

Coconut milk adds a pleasant, exotic flavor, and if you appreciate its taste, you can replace up to one-third of the rice milk with it. The dried pineapple can be exchanged for dried apricots, dried mango, candied fruits, or prunes.

■ Pour the rice flakes into a bowl. Add the rice milk and coconut milk and let the rice flakes rest for 15 minutes to absorb the liquid. Add the dried pineapple and raisins. Then stir in the sugar and mix in the eggs.

■ Slice the fresh fruits and mix them into the batter. Pour into a well-oiled cake pan and bake at 425 degrees Fahrenheit for 30 to 40 minutes (depending upon the pan used and the thickness of the pudding).

Chestnut Pudding

1 (14-ounce) can whole chestnuts

2 eggs

7 tablespoons quinoa flour

¼ cup raw cane sugar

⅓ cup chocolate chips

¾ teaspoon baking powder

A treat for lovers of chestnut cream, this pudding can be prepared in under ten minutes. The melt-in-your-mouth texture is wonderful with a few chocolate chips, which sweeten the batter.

■ Purée the chestnuts with their liquid in a food processor until smooth. Transfer to a bowl and mix in the eggs. Add the quinoa flour, sugar, chocolate chips, and baking powder.

■ Pour into an oiled cake pan and bake at 400–425 degrees Fahrenheit for 25 minutes. Let cool before serving.

Chestnut Pudding with Dried Fruit: Omit the chocolate chips and add a handful of golden raisins or 5 or 6 pitted prunes cut into small pieces.

Peach Crumble with Crunchy Rice Topping >

Eat this dessert warm or cold and savor the peach-flavored fondant beneath the rice flake crust. This same recipe will be equally delicious if you replace the peaches with fresh figs.

8 peaches

1/2 cup raw cane sugar

7 tablespoons vegetable margarine, softened

1 3/4 cups rice flakes, toasted

1/2 cup diced dried apples

3 tablespoons sesame seeds

- Coat a baking pan with margarine. Cut the peaches into slices and arrange them in the pan.

- Combine the sugar and margarine in a bowl. Add the rice flakes, dried apples, and sesame seeds. Scatter over the peaches. Bake at 375 degrees Fahrenheit for 25 minutes.

Banana Pudding with Cinnamon Sauce

In this eggless pudding with rice flakes, it's the bananas that allow the mixture to thicken. I often serve it with crème anglaise or a fruit coulis.

Banana Pudding

1 1/2 cups rice flakes

1 1/4 cups rice milk

2 bananas

1/4 cup organic dark brown sugar

1 handful (about 3 tablespoons) raisins

- To make the pudding, place the rice flakes and rice milk into a bowl. Let the rice flakes soak up the milk while you mash the bananas on a plate with a fork. Add the mashed bananas to the rice flakes and mix in the sugar and raisins.

- Pour into an oiled cake pan, and bake at 400 degrees Fahrenheit for 30 to 35 minutes. Let cool if you wish to remove it from the pan, or cut directly into slices if you want to leave it in the pan.

Cinnamon Sauce

1 tablespoon plus 1 teaspoon cream of rice (farina)

1/2 teaspoon ground cinnamon

1 1/4 cups vanilla soymilk

3 tablespoons agave syrup, more or less as needed

- To make the cinnamon sauce, place the cream of rice and cinnamon in a small saucepan. Thin with the soymilk. Place over low heat and stir constantly until thickened. The cream should coat the spoon while remaining fluid.

- Remove from heat and add agave syrup to taste. Pour into a dish and place in the refrigerator. The sauce will become creamy as it cools.

Millet Semolina Gratin with Fruit Preserves   >

A dessert you will choose in any season! You can garnish it any way you like: with prunes, dried apricots, apple slices, grated coconut, dates, raisins, or bits of pear.

■ Put the millet semolina in a saucepan and add the almond milk. Place over low heat. As soon as it starts to simmer, add the marmalade and stir constantly, as the mixture will begin to thicken. Cook for 1 minute. Remove from the heat and add the apples. Cool until the mixture is barely warm (so the eggs won't set). Then add the eggs, one at a time.

■ Oil a small gratin dish or several individual ramekins. Pour in the mixture and bake at 400 degrees Fahrenheit for 25 minutes. Enjoy warm or cold.

¾ cup fine millet semolina

2 cups almond milk, rice milk, or soymilk

3 to 5 tablespoons orange marmalade, cherry preserves, or apricot preserves

2 apples, peeled and thinly sliced

2 eggs

Coconut Crisp

This dessert combines a compote of rhubarb, mellowed by bananas and sweetened with raisins, with a crusty coconut topping similar to a crumble. The rhubarb stalks are cut into segments and stewed beforehand with a little sugar to reduce some of their acidity.

■ Peel the rhubarb, removing the strings, and cut into segments. Place into a thick-bottomed saucepan with the bananas, and cook over low heat for 15 minutes. If the compote is very sour, add a little rice syrup or sugar.

■ While the compote is cooking, mix the margarine with the sugar and rice flour in a bowl. Add the grated coconut, using just as much as is needed to make a sandy, granular topping.

■ Add the raisins to the rhubarb-banana compote and pour into an oiled ovenproof dish. Cover the compote with the coconut mixture.

■ Place under the broiler for 10 to 15 minutes, allowing the topping to turn golden brown. Enjoy cold or slightly warm.

6 to 8 rhubarb stalks

2 bananas, sliced

Rice syrup or raw cane sugar (optional)

3½ tablespoons vegetable margarine, softened

3 tablespoons organic dark brown sugar

2 tablespoons rice flour

Grated coconut, as needed

1 handful (about 3 tablespoons) raisins

Note: This recipe makes 6 servings.

< Tutti Frutti Crumble

6 peaches, preferably of
different varieties

2 or 3 apricots

Prunes

1 1/2 cups finely ground
almonds

1/2 cup raw cane sugar

1 teaspoon ground cinnamon

The "crumble" is made of finely ground almonds mixed with sugar and cinnamon. As the summer goes by, it's simple to transform this dessert with whatever fruits are in season.

■ To prepare a fruit compote, cut all the fruit into slices or small cubes. Place it in a saucepan over low heat and cook briefly.

■ Meanwhile, mix the finely ground almonds with the sugar and cinnamon. Pour the compote in an oiled ovenproof dish. Sprinkle the almond mixture over the fruit.

■ Bake at 400-425 degrees Fahrenheit for about 15 minutes, just until the crumble turns golden brown.

Apple Crumble with Chestnut Flour

8 apples, peeled and diced

2 tablespoons freshly
squeezed lemon juice

1/3 cup vegetable margarine,
softened

3/4 cup raw cane sugar

2 1/2 cups chestnut flour

1 teaspoon ground cinnamon

Chestnut flour flavored with cinnamon and sugar makes a shortbread topping that complements stewed fruit.

■ Put the apples into a saucepan. Sprinkle the lemon juice over them and toss. Cook over low heat until the mixture forms a compote.

■ To make a crumble topping, mix the margarine and sugar in a bowl. Add the chestnut flour and cinnamon and mix well to obtain a sandy, granular texture. Alternatively, process the ingredients in a food processor until the texture is similar to coarse semolina.

■ Spread the compote in an ovenproof dish coated with margarine. Sprinkle the crumble topping over the fruit and tamp it down. Bake at 400–425 degrees Fahrenheit for 10 to 15 minutes.

Chocolate and Hazelnut Gratin >

Serve this gratin in a large, ovenproof dish or in several individual round earthenware ramekins, like a flan or crème brûlée.

■ Toast the chestnut flour in a skillet over low heat until it just starts to brown. Watch closely so it doesn't burn! Remove from the heat and transfer to a medium saucepan. Add the rice milk and chocolate and warm over low heat until the chocolate is melted. Remove from the heat and stir in the ground hazelnuts. The batter will be quite thin (as the gratin bakes, the chestnut flour will expand and absorb the liquid).

■ Pour into an oiled baking dish and bake at 400–425 degrees Fahrenheit for 15 to 20 minutes (watch closely so it does not burn!). Cool completely before serving.

1 cup chestnut flour

2 cups rice milk

1.75 ounces dark chocolate, broken into pieces

1 cup finely ground hazelnuts

Banana Gratin with Cardamom

A quick and easy dessert to prepare, it can be served in small individual gratin cups.

■ Place the rice flour in a small saucepan. Stir in the rice milk and coconut cream. Cook and stir over low heat until thickened. The mixture should be the consistency of pastry cream. Sweeten with the maple syrup.

■ Peel the bananas and mash them with a fork. Mix the banana purée with the thickened cream and pour into an oiled ovenproof dish. Sprinkle with the ground almonds and cardamom. Place under the broiler for less than 10 minutes. Let cool before serving.

Note: Don't confuse coconut cream with the sweetened product used for making drinks. To get coconut cream, place a can of full-fat coconut milk in the refrigerator for at least 2 hours. Take care to keep the can upright, and do not shake it while opening. Scoop the solid cream off the top (about one-third to one-half of the can will turn into solid cream).

4 tablespoons rice flour

2/3 cup rice milk

6 tablespoons coconut cream (see note)

4 tablespoons maple syrup

4 bananas

3 tablespoons finely ground blanched almonds

1/2 teaspoon ground cardamom

Making cookies and small cakes ... without gluten

A selection of small cookies

■ Madeleines (made with rice flour), Coconut Balls, Chestnut Brownies, Green Matcha Tea Cakes with Pistachios... all these treats are easy to take along for get-togethers.

■ Multiply these recipes by choosing the cake batters you prefer: is it the Hazelnut Cake with Almond Cream (page 44), the Yogurt Cake (page 52), or the Cinnamon Marble Cake (page 41). Bake the batter of your choice in cupcake tins, or in mini cake pans. Serving small individual cakes offers a different taste and appeal.

■ You can enrich these basic cake batters with walnuts, hazelnuts, chocolate chips, raisins, or dried fruits (be careful when you shop, as some can be powdered with flour!). For an alternative to chocolate with bread, add squares of a chocolate bar when you pour the batter into the tins.

Snacks

For snacks, think about the possibilities of dried fruits—prunes, apricots, raisins—and richer foods. Almonds and hazelnuts can be put on a baking sheet and placed under the broiler to be lightly toasted, which will give them a slightly different flavor.

Cookies and Small Cakes

Green Matcha Tea Cakes with Pistachios >

Matcha tea is a powdered green Japanese tea (when organic, it comes from Thailand). Incorporated into a cake batter, it gives a brilliant green color and imparts the natural flavor of fresh green tea.

9 tablespoons vegetable margarine

2/3 cup raw cane sugar

3/4 cup rice flour

2 tablespoons matcha tea

1 teaspoon baking powder

4 eggs

3/4 cup chopped unsalted pistachios

■ Melt the margarine in a saucepan over low heat. Remove from the heat and add the sugar. Then stir in the rice flour, matcha tea, and baking powder. Add the eggs, one at a time, and mix well after each addition.

■ Pour into individual mini cake pans or muffin tins that have been coated with margarine. Sprinkle the pistachios over the batter. Bake at 425 degrees Fahrenheit for 10 to 15 minutes, depending on the size of the pans. Remove from the pans while still warm.

Caramel and Coconut Spiced Macaroons >>

Baked in lined cupcake pans, these macaroons are like spice loaves and have a slight flavor of caramel from the raw cane sugar. The anise seeds lend a fresh flavor; if you prefer, you can substitute orange zest for a variation that's more warm and fruity.

1/4 cup coconut cream (see note)

1/3 cup organic dark brown sugar

1 cup rice flour

1 teaspoon baking powder

1 teaspoon ground cinnamon

1/2 teaspoon ground cardamom

1 pinch anise seeds

1 pinch orange zest (optional)

■ Put the coconut cream into a bowl and stir until it is smooth. Stir in the sugar. Then add the rice flour, baking powder, cinnamon, cardamom, anise seeds, and optional orange zest. Mix well to form a thick dough that can be rolled into a ball.

■ Divide into 6 to 8 equal portions, and roll them rapidly between the palms of your hands to form balls about the size of an apricot. Flatten the balls slightly and place them in mini pans that are lined with paper muffin cups. Bake at 400–425 degrees Fahrenheit for 20 to 25 minutes.

Note: Don't confuse coconut cream with the sweetened product used for making drinks. To get coconut cream, place a can of full-fat coconut milk in the refrigerator for at least 2 hours. Take care to keep the can upright, and do not shake it while opening. Scoop the solid cream off the top (about one-third to one-half of the can will turn into solid cream).

Caramel and Coconut
Spiced Macaroons

Chestnut Brownies >

Warning to gourmands: these moist brownies are even better the next day—if you can wait!

■ Toast the chestnut flour in a small skillet over low heat until just brown. Watch closely so it doesn't burn! Remove from the heat and immediately transfer to a saucepan. Add the chocolate, margarine, and sugar. Warm over low heat, just until the chocolate and margarine are melted. Remove from the heat and let cool for 5 to 10 minutes. Add the egg yolks, one at a time. Mix carefully.

■ Beat the egg whites until stiff, and fold them into the chocolate mixture. Fold in the walnuts.

■ Pour into an 8 x 8-inch pan or a layer cake pan (for thicker brownies) that has been lined with parchment paper and bake at 400–425 degrees Fahrenheit for 25 minutes. Let cool, then cut into large squares.

$1/3$ cup chestnut flour

3.5 ounces dark chocolate, broken into pieces

7 tablespoons vegetable margarine

$6\frac{1}{2}$ tablespoons raw cane sugar

4 eggs, separated

$1/2$ cup walnuts

Coconut Balls

Rice syrup lightly sweetens this mixture, while the cream of rice binds it as it cooks. Cream of rice is a dry farina that has been precooked.

■ Combine the coconut and rice syrup in a bowl. Add the cream of rice and mix well. Place about 10 small mounds of the mixture on an oiled baking sheet.

■ Bake at 400 degrees Fahrenheit for 10 to 15 minutes. The more the balls brown, the crispier they will be. If you prefer them softer in the center, don't let them turn brown. Remove from the baking sheet and let cool.

$1\frac{1}{4}$ cups grated coconut

$6\frac{1}{2}$ tablespoons rice syrup

$3\frac{1}{2}$ tablespoons cream of rice (farina)

Snack-Time Madeleines

Light and flavorful madeleines, delicious with tea for a gourmand's breakfast or a comforting snack.

¾ cup raw cane sugar

9 tablespoons vegetable margarine, softened

2 eggs

1 cup rice flour

1 teaspoon baking powder

5 drops grapefruit essential oil, or 5 drops bergamot essential oil and ½ teaspoon lemon zest, for flavoring

Note: This recipe makes 6 servings.

■ Preheat the oven to 400–425 degrees Fahrenheit. Cream together the sugar and margarine. Add the eggs. Then add the rice flour and baking powder. Stir in the grapefruit essential oil.

■ Pour into well-oiled madeleine pans; don't fill them completely to the top. Watch them carefully as they bake; as soon as the madeleines are golden brown and form a peak they are nearly done. Remove them from the pan while still warm (in order to get them out easily).

Note: If you use an organic dark brown sugar in place of the cane sugar, flavor the madeleines with ½ teaspoon ground cinnamon or with orange zest.

Petite Date Cookies

Sweetened with rice syrup and dates, which become chewy when baked, these small cookies make great snacks that are easy to take along.

1 cup rice flour

1 cup buckwheat flour

⅓ cup chopped almonds

1 teaspoon baking powder

⅓ cup light olive oil

⅓ cup rice milk

5 tablespoons rice syrup or honey

10 pitted dates, cut into small pieces

Note: This recipe makes about 10 cookies.

■ Combine the rice flour, buckwheat flour, almonds, and baking powder in a bowl. Add the oil, rice milk, and rice syrup. Add the dates to the dough, which should be quite thick.

■ Using a spoon and a spatula, place small mounds, about the size of a large nut, on a lined baking sheet. Flatten them slightly with the back of a spoon. Bake at 425 degrees Fahrenheit for 25 minutes, until lightly browned.

Coconut Cakes >

Moist and half-covered in a chocolate glaze, these little cakes please young and old alike. Good as a dessert or snack.

■ Preheat the oven to 425 degrees Fahrenheit. Combine the coconut and sugar in a bowl and mix in the egg whites. Add the flour and baking powder. Pour into a well-oiled madeleine pan (or cupcake pan). Bake for 10 minutes at 425 degrees, then lower the heat to 400 degrees for an additional 10 minutes to finish baking.

■ Melt the chocolate with the rice milk in a small saucepan. Remove the little cakes from the pan and dip half of each one into the melted chocolate. Let cool on a rack.

1 cup grated coconut

¾ cup raw cane sugar

2 egg whites

⅓ cup rice flour

1 teaspoon baking powder

3.5 ounces dark chocolate

5 to 6 tablespoons rice milk

Note: This recipe makes 12 small cakes.

Grapefruit-Flavored Mini Cakes

These little flourless cakes are full of chewy almonds. To vary the flavor, you can replace the grapefruit essential oil with lemon zest. They're delicious with crémes, flans, compotes... and tea!

■ Combine the egg yolks and the ground almonds in a bowl. Stir in the grapefruit essential oil. In a separate bowl, place the egg whites and confectioners' sugar and whip into soft peaks. Fold one spoonful of egg whites into the almond mixture and mix well. Then add the remainder of the egg whites, a little at a time.

■ Fill (but not all the way to the top) rectangular mini cake pans that have been well oiled. Bake at 400 degrees Fahrenheit for 10 to 15 minutes. Watch closely; when they are golden, they are nearly done. Remove from the pans while still warm. Let cool completely before eating.

4 eggs, separated

1 cup finely ground blanched almonds

6 drops grapefruit essential oil

½ cup confectioners' sugar

Note: This recipe makes 15 small cakes.

Autumn Shortbread Cookies

These tender cookies are flavored with hazelnuts and chestnuts. The dough is baked on a sheet and cut into squares when finished.

■ To make a hazelnut purée, place the hazelnuts in a saucepan and cover with water. Bring to a boil, lower the heat, and simmer for 30 minutes. Do not drain (keeping them moist will help the skins come off more easily and prevent the nuts from drying out). Let cool just until the nuts can be easily handled. While the nuts are still warm, remove as much of the brown skin as possible. Drain lightly, transfer to a food processor, and purée until smooth.

■ Put the hazelnut purée into a bowl and add the remaining ingredients. Mix well to make a soft dough. Line a cookie sheet with parchment paper and spread the dough on it, with the aid of a spatula, to slightly less than ½ inch thick.

■ Bake at 400–425 degrees Fahrenheit for 20 minutes. The dough should just barely turn golden brown; do not over-bake. Remove from the oven and cut into 1-inch squares. Let cool.

Variation: Stir a handful of chocolate chips or ground hazelnuts into the dough.

¼ cup hazelnuts

1⅔ cups chestnut flour

1 cup finely ground almonds

2 eggs

6½ tablespoons raw cane sugar

2 tablespoons olive oil

Vanilla extract (optional)

Crêpes

Sugar or Honey Crêpes

>

The subtle flavor of quinoa transforms this batter, which produces slightly puffed crêpes. Serve them with compotes, fruit marmalades, a praline topping, rice syrup, or honey.

■ Combine the rice flour and quinoa flour in a bowl. Add the eggs, then stir in the soymilk, a little at a time. Let rest for 2 hours. If the batter seems a bit thick, add a little more soymilk.

■ To cook, heat a well-oiled crêpe pan and pour in a ladleful of batter. As soon as the first side is browned, flip it over.

1/3 cup rice flour

1/4 cup quinoa flour

2 eggs

3/4 cup soymilk

Rice Flour and Almond Milk Crêpes

This batter makes light, delicately flavored crêpes. Cover them with your choice of citrus jellies, chocolate sauce, chestnut cream, or honey.

■ Put the flour and sugar into a bowl. Add the eggs and mandarin essential oil. Stir vigorously. Then stir in the almond milk.

■ Allow the batter to rest for 15 to 30 minutes. In order for the crêpes to be moist and slightly puffy, cook them in a well-oiled, heated crêpe pan.

1/2 cup rice flour

1 tablespoon raw cane sugar

2 eggs

3 drops mandarin essential oil

2/3 cup almond milk or chestnut milk

Note: This recipe makes 6 crêpes.

Praline and Cocoa Blinis

¼ cup hazelnuts
or almonds

¼ cup organic dark
brown sugar

1¼ cups rice flour

2 tablespoons cocoa powder

3 eggs

1 cup hazelnut milk or
almond milk

*Note: This recipe makes
about 12 blinis.*

Serve these mini crêpes with a bowl of vanilla ice cream, cocoa sorbet, or chocolate sauce, or spread them with hazelnut butter.

■ Place the hazelnuts in a zipper-lock plastic bag. Press to remove all the air, seal, and crush the nuts with a rolling pin. Transfer to a small skillet and toast over low heat for about 5 minutes. Add the brown sugar and continue to toast until the mixture becomes crumbly.

■ Transfer to a bowl and add the flour and cocoa powder. Add the eggs and mix well. Stir in the hazelnut milk.

■ Oil and heat a small blini pan, griddle, or skillet. When the pan is hot, add a ladleful of the batter, then immediately rotate the pan gently to allow the batter to spread thin. Turn over the mini crêpe as soon as it is firm enough to be easily flipped. Cook the remaining batter in the same fashion. Serve immediately.

Note: This recipe makes about 12 blinis.

Chestnut Flour Griddle Cakes

1½ cups chestnut flour
(sift, if lumpy)

1 cup buckwheat flour

2 cups plus 2 tablespoons
soymilk

This batter produces moist, airy crêpes. They're delicious with a nut-based cream or a chocolate sauce, as well as with flambéed apples, honey, or ground hazelnuts.

■ Combine the chestnut flour and buckwheat flour in a bowl. Stir in the soymilk.

■ To cook, ladle the batter onto a well-oiled and heated crêpe pan. If the first crêpe is a little underdone, the following ones will be perfect when the pan is the right temperature.

Notes: The soymilk gives a good texture, but it can be replaced with rice milk, if you prefer.

The batter needs to be a little thick; don't make the griddle cakes too thin.

There is no need to let the batter rest. In addition, after a day or two, it will ferment and taste bitter.

Creamy desserts ...
without gluten

The sweetness in these creamy desserts comes from puréed nuts, which are rich in natural fats. They are crushed slowly and evenly by millstones until they are transformed into a fine paste. Then the spreadable paste, plain or sweetened, is packaged in containers.

Purées of hazelnuts and blanched or raw almonds mix best with sweet flavors. In addition to their nutritional qualities, these naturally tasty ingredients add good flavor to pastry doughs and batters. Puréed blanched almonds make a sweet paste that can be added to creams, zabaglione, and other desserts. Raw (unblanched) almonds and hazelnuts are stronger in flavor.

Mixed with honey or rice syrup, these purées will allow you to make fillings for génoises (sponge cakes) or birthday cakes, or you can use them as fillings for cookies or as spreads. Thin raw almond purée with maple syrup or agave syrup and use it as a frosting for shortbread cookies. These rich creams can be turned into vegetable milks if you dilute them with a small amount of barely warm water.

What is agar-agar?

Agar-agar is a natural gelatin extracted from certain seaweeds. It can be found powdered or in ready-to-use flakes. It's a very healthful and mild gelatin (it has a protective effect on the intestines). With its neutral flavor, this ingredient is easy to use in cooking to gel flans, Bavarian cream, and preserves.

Creamy Desserts

Rice Cream with Orange Flower Water   >

This special rice cream, prepared with almond or rice milk, produces quite a light dessert. I serve it in glasses or in small jam jars with lids, which makes a practical way to prepare it ahead of time and keep it in the refrigerator.

- Place the rice in a saucepan, and pour the water over it. Simmer over very low heat for 25 minutes, just until the liquid is absorbed. Remove from the heat and add the rice milk, rice syrup, and orange flower water. Mix well, cover, and allow the rice to swell.

- Pour into glass containers and sprinkle with the slivered almonds. Cover and chill in the refrigerator or enjoy while still warm.

2/3 cup white rice

1 1/2 cups water

1/2 cup rice milk or almond milk

4 tablespoons rice syrup

1 tablespoon orange flower water

1 handful (about 3 tablespoons) slivered almonds

Coconut Cream Fondant

This cream should be prepared at least two hours in advance so it can thicken in the refrigerator.

- Place the coconut cream and coconut oil in a saucepan and warm over very low heat. Add the sugar. Split the vanilla bean in two and scrape out the seeds with the point of a knife. Add the seeds to the coconut cream.

- Place the cream of rice in a small bowl and mix in the rice milk. Add it to the coconut cream. Cook over low heat, stirring constantly, for 5 minutes, until slightly thickened and smooth. Pour into individual ramekins and chill in the refrigerator.

- A few minutes before serving, put the grated coconut into a sauté pan and brown it over low heat (this will take just a few seconds). Sprinkle the browned coconut over the coconut cream and serve.

Note: Don't confuse coconut cream with the sweetened product used for making drinks. To get coconut cream, place a can of full-fat coconut milk in the refrigerator for at least 2 hours. Take care to keep the can upright, and do not shake it while opening. Scoop the solid cream off the top (about one-third to one-half of the can will turn into solid cream).

1/2 cup coconut cream (see note)

1/4 cup coconut oil

4 tablespoons raw cane sugar

1 vanilla bean

3 tablespoons cream of rice (farina)

2/3 cup rice milk

2 tablespoons grated coconut

Pineapple Crème Brûlée >

An exotic flavor infuses this quick and easy dessert. Serve it for special occasions.

■ Preheat the oven to 400 degrees Fahrenheit, and oil a gratin dish or 4 small ovenproof dishes, for individual servings.

■ Put the pineapple into the food processor. Add the eggs, rice flour, and sugar, and process until well combined. Pour into the prepared dish (or dishes) and bake for 20 minutes. Enjoy warm for a creamy consistency, or place it in the refrigerator to savor a thicker, more fondant-like cream.

2 cups diced fresh pineapple

3 eggs

3 tablespoons rice flour

2½ tablespoons organic dark brown sugar

Almond and Chestnut Cream

A truly easy recipe that is very pleasing, this cream can be served in dessert glasses or as an accompaniment to brownies or chocolate cake. For the best results, use a thick, rich almond milk.

■ Sift the chestnut flour to remove any lumps. Transfer it to a saucepan, and stir in the almond milk, a little at a time, until smooth. Place over low heat, stirring constantly, until thickened.

■ Add the honey and continue to cook, stirring constantly, for 5 minutes longer. Pour into dessert dishes, and chill before serving.

¾ cup chestnut flour

1 quart almond milk

3 to 5 tablespoons honey or maple syrup

Flower Water Gel >

This gel uses agar-agar, a sea vegetable, rather than bovine gelatin, and almond or rice milk, which adds sweetness. The vegetable milk combines well with the subtle perfume of the flower water, which is added last for flavor. Simple and fast, this gel can be prepared ahead of time.

2 cups rice milk or almond milk

2 teaspoons agar-agar powder

2 tablespoons raw cane sugar

2 tablespoons flower water (see note)

■ Pour the rice milk into a medium saucepan. Add the agar-agar powder and sugar and bring to a simmer over low heat. Cook and stir for 2 to 3 minutes. Remove from the heat and stir in the flower water.

■ Immediately pour into dessert glasses. Chill thoroughly before serving. Serve cold.

Note: To make flower water, add 1 teaspoon dried flower petals (make sure the flower is edible) to ¼ cup boiling water. Let steep for 5 min, and then strain out the petals. Lavender, rose, and lemon verbena are good choices.

Warning: Rose water bought at a store, unless specifically designated as a food ingredient, is likely not edible and may be glycerin based.

Chocolate Chestnut Supreme

Quick to prepare ahead of time, this terrine of almond cream and chocolate is fondant-like and light at the same time. If you use little sugar in your desserts, the chocolate squares mixed into the vegetable milk and chestnut purée will be sufficient. But if you prefer a sweeter flavor, choose a vegetable milk that is already sweetened and flavored (such as vanilla, almond, or hazelnut).

1 (14-ounce) can whole chestnuts

1 cup rice milk, soymilk, or almond milk

3.5 ounces dark chocolate

1 teaspoon agar-agar powder

■ Purée the chestnuts with their liquid in the food processor until smooth. Transfer to a bowl.

■ Put the rice milk and chocolate into a saucepan. Sprinkle with the agar-agar powder. Place over low heat and simmer very gently for 3 minutes, stirring constantly. Pour over the puréed chestnuts in increments, while stirring well. Immediately fill a bread pan or fruitcake pan (use a glass or porcelain pan to be able to remove the slices more easily) and place in the refrigerator overnight. For quicker setting, fill individual dessert glasses.

Raspberry Cup   >

Here is a quick and creamy dessert. You can add soy cream at the end of cooking to make it even smoother.
In order to not overpower the flavor of the raspberries, a light-flavored agave syrup is used.

■ Combine the millet semolina and rice milk in a saucepan and place over low heat. As soon as the mixture begins to simmer, stir constantly, since it will thicken quickly (in about 1 minute). For a smoother, creamier mixture, stir in the optional soy cream.

■ Remove from the heat and stir in the agave syrup. Place a layer of the raspberry coulis in the bottom of dessert glasses before spooning in the semolina mixture. Chill before serving.

Variation: An equal amount of other fruit purées, such as apricot, rhubarb, or cherry, may be used in place of the raspberry coulis.

3/4 cup millet semolina

1 cup plus 2 tablespoons rice milk or soymilk

1/3 cup soy cream (optional)

5 tablespoons agave syrup or rice syrup

1 cup raspberry coulis (blended raspberries)

Chocolate Amaranth

Surprise your dinner guests with an amaranth dessert. These tiny grains (even smaller than quinoa) are nutrient rich.

■ Combine the amaranth and water in a saucepan and bring to a boil. Reduce the heat to low and simmer until the water is completely absorbed, about 30 minutes. Remove from the heat, cover, and let the grains swell. Upon cooling, the small grains thicken to a texture similar to cooked semolina.

■ While the amaranth is cooking, make a hazelnut purée. Place the hazelnuts in a saucepan and cover with water. Bring to a boil, lower the heat, and simmer for 30 minutes. Do not drain (keeping them moist will help the skins come off more easily and prevent the nuts from drying out). Let cool just until the nuts can be easily handled. While the nuts are still warm, remove as much of the brown skin as possible. Drain lightly, transfer to a food processor, and purée until smooth.

■ Place the chocolate in a saucepan with a few spoonfuls of water. Melt over very low heat. Add the rice syrup and the puréed hazelnuts. Stir well and mix in the amaranth.

■ Remove from the heat and mix vigorously. Stir in the chopped almonds. Spoon into dessert glasses and refrigerate until ready to serve.

1/2 cup amaranth

1 1/4 cups water

3 tablespoons hazelnuts

3.5 ounces chocolate, broken into pieces

4 tablespoons rice syrup

1 handful (about 3 tablespoons) coarsely chopped almonds

Chestnut English Cream

<

4 egg yolks

6½ tablespoons organic dark brown sugar

⅔ cup chestnut meal (coarsely ground cooked chestnuts)

3¾ cups rice milk

6 drops orange essential oil

Note: This recipe makes 6 servings.

A cream to accompany dry cookies, chestnut cakes, or chocolate fondant. The orange flavor combines well with the sweetness of the chestnuts. If you prefer, in place of essential oil, use orange zest.

■ Combine the egg yolks and sugar in a saucepan. Add the chestnut meal and mix in the rice milk, a little at a time. Place over low heat and stir just until the cream thickens and coats the spoon. Add the essential oil.

■ Remove from heat, pour into dessert glasses, and let cool.

Frangipane of Orange-Flavored Prunes >>

2 cups pitted prunes

⅔ cup orange flower water

2 egg yolks

3 tablespoons organic dark brown sugar

¼ cup rice flour

1 cup plus 2 tablespoons rice milk or almond milk

2 to 3 tablespoons almond butter

This frangipane is based on a pastry cream and contains prunes steeped in orange flower water. These should be prepared the night before or several hours before the meal. The frangipane cream can serve just as well as a garnish for a tart or cake.

■ The night before, put the prunes and orange flower water into a bowl, and add enough plain water to cover the prunes. Let steep overnight.

■ To prepare the frangipane cream, combine the egg yolks and sugar in a small saucepan. Add the rice flour and rice milk and place over low heat, stirring briskly, just until the cream thickens. Remove from heat and stir in the almond butter. Pour into dessert glasses and let cool.

■ When it's time for dessert, drain the prunes and place some on top of each serving. The orange flower-flavored water can be served as a beverage.

Frangipane of Orange-
Flavored Prunes

Tapioca Mysteries with Date Syrup >

Date syrup is packaged in glass jars. Its flavor is sweet and aromatic. Brown in color, this very dark syrup resembles a chocolate sauce and makes a lovely contrast and a tasty surprise for this upside-down tapioca dessert.

■ Combine the rice milk and tapioca in a saucepan and place over a low flame. Add the sugar and vanilla bean. Let simmer over low heat for 5 to 10 minutes, stirring frequently, just until the tapioca thickens. The mixture should be thick and translucent. Remove the vanilla bean.

■ Pour 1 to 2 spoonfuls of date syrup into the bottom of several coffee cups (or choose dessert glasses that will give a dome shape) and fill with the tapioca. Refrigerate. As it cools, the mixture will gel.

■ After several hours, when the tapioca is well set, run the blade of a tableware knife around the sides of each cup. Remove the tapioca and transfer it to individual dessert plates. Stick a small piece of vanilla bean into each pyramid.

Note: You can reduce the amount of sugar if you use a milk that is already flavored with vanilla.

Variation: You can create other desserts by replacing the date syrup with cherry, apricot, or raspberry preserves.

2½ cups rice milk or soymilk

1 cup tapioca

4 tablespoons raw cane sugar

½ vanilla bean, split in half lengthwise

Date syrup (see note)

Note: If you cannot find bottled date syrup, you can make your own. Place pitted dates in a saucepan and cover them with water or freshly squeezed orange juice. Bring to a boil, then reduce the heat and simmer for 30 minutes. Process the dates and liquid in a blender until smooth, adding additional water, if needed, to make a thick syrup.

Four-Spice Chocolate Flan

Light, thanks to the agar-agar, this chocolate flan can be prepared quickly. It's especially good with madeleines and other small cakes or cookies.

■ Combine the sugar, cocoa, agar-agar powder, and four-spice powder in a saucepan. Stir in the soymilk. Add the vanilla bean, if using, and place over low heat. Simmer for 3 minutes while stirring constantly.

■ Pour the mixture into individual ramekins or into a dessert bowl. Refrigerate at least 2 hours before serving.

2 tablespoons raw cane sugar

2 tablespoons cocoa powder

1 teaspoon agar-agar powder

1 pinch four-spice powder or ground cinnamon

2 cups plus 2 tablespoons vanilla soymilk (unsweetened)

½ vanilla bean, split in half lengthwise (optional)

Vanilla Pastry Cream

This pastry cream can be used as the basis for many delicious recipes. Its vanilla flavor goes well with everything. If you wish to add a subtle caramel flavor, replace the raw cane sugar with organic dark brown sugar.

4 egg yolks

6½ tablespoons raw cane sugar

½ cup rice flour

2½ cups rice milk or soymilk

1 vanilla bean

■ Combine the egg yolks and sugar in a small saucepan. Add the rice flour and stir in the rice milk. Split the vanilla bean in half lengthwise and remove the center part with the tip of a knife; mix it into the milk mixture.

■ Place over low heat, stirring constantly, just until it thickens. The cream is ready to garnish a tart or a cake, or pour it into dessert glasses to enjoy cold as a dessert.

Light Breakfasts

Light breakfasts ...

Spring Breakfasts

■ A fresh and rich recipe: mash a ripe banana and mix it into all-natural soy yogurt. Add a tablespoon of this creamed mixture to gluten-free sprouted grains or seeds and half an apple, cut into thin slices.

■ When strawberry season arrives, prepare a fruit salad accompanied by a creamy cereal made with rice flour or cooked quinoa or rice, mixed with vegetable milk and cooked over low heat until thickened. Sweeten this cream lightly with rice syrup (if you prefer a sweetener that is absorbed slowly by the body) or a little raw sugar. You can also use almond milk or rice milk that is already sweetened. These creamy mixtures can be prepared in less than 15 minutes, or made the night before in order to enjoy a breakfast that is ready to eat in the morning.

Summer Breakfasts

■ Think about brightly colored fruit salads: yellow and white peaches, raspberries, apricots... Take advantage of vacation time to prepare light rice or quinoa cream puddings, desserts made with rice semolina, or tapioca flan... This is the time to familiarize yourself with different ingredients, to taste and test recipes that will become your favorites. A clafoutis made in advance with rice meal, peaches, plums, or apricots will turn your breakfast into a treat!

■ To enjoy tarts with marmalade made from fruits of the season (apricots, rhubarb, blueberries, or raspberry and currant jelly), prepare brioches or cakes with less sugar.

... without gluten

Autumn Breakfasts

■ Celebrate with madeleines and slices of cake that you have made in advance. Make delicious creams with chestnut flour or chestnut milk, and flavor them with puréed hazelnuts or almonds.

■ Think about soaking dried fruit (such as prunes or raisins) the night before, and then mix them with sliced apples or pears for a fruit salad. Enjoyed while still warm or slightly cooled, Almond and Chestnut Cream (page 114) will certainly be appreciated on a chilly early morning.

Winter Breakfasts

■ Get organized the night before by preparing a crêpe batter made with vegetable milk and chestnut flour. In the morning, the crêpes are quickly made and the toppings are so appetizing: hazelnut or raw almond purée, honey, or melted chocolate.

■ This is the time to taste big, moist cakes made with carrots or pumpkin, and to prepare chestnut cream or banana pudding. Serve them with a compote of apples, pears, or quince.

Good Morning Cream Pudding

2 ounces cream of rice (farina)

1 cup plus 2 tablespoons almond milk, hazelnut milk, rice milk, or soymilk

1 heaping tablespoon raw almond butter

3 to 4 tablespoons agave syrup or rice syrup

1 handful sprouted sunflower seeds or quinoa

Diced dried apples

Raisins (optional)

Take advantage of the energy-generating properties of germinated seeds to brighten your mornings with this cream pudding that you can prepare in just a few minutes. Enjoy the light, sweet taste.

■ Put the cream of rice into a saucepan and add the almond milk, a little at a time. Place over low heat and simmer for 5 minutes, stirring constantly, until thickened.

■ Remove from the heat and add the almond butter. Mix well so that it melts into the warm, creamy mixture. Sweeten to taste with the agave syrup.

■ Pour into dessert glasses and sprinkle with the sprouted seeds, dried apples, and optional raisins.

Chocolate Quinoa Cream Pudding

7 tablespoons quinoa flour

2 tablespoons raw cane sugar, maple syrup, or agave syrup

2 tablespoons cocoa powder

1 ⅓ cups rice milk or almond milk

3 drops orange essential oil

This chocolaty, creamy breakfast can also serve as a snack or dessert. If you decide to substitute syrup for the sugar, add it after cooking, as it tends to get bitter when heated.

■ Combine the quinoa flour, sugar, and cocoa powder in a saucepan. Gradually stir in the rice milk, a little at a time. Cook on low heat, stirring constantly.

■ If serving hot, remove from the heat as soon as it starts to thicken, and spoon into dessert glasses. If you want to serve it cold, allow it to thicken longer, being careful not to burn it. This pudding will actually become thinner in the refrigerator instead of thicker. Add the essential oil when you remove the pudding from the heat.

Quinoa Muesli >

A sweet, chewy breakfast treat that allows you to savor the moment while enjoying the fruits of the season.

■ Combine the quinoa, water, chopped pears, and raisins in a saucepan. Cover and cook on low heat for 15 minutes.

■ Just before serving, add the vegetable milk, drizzle with syrup, and sprinkle with the cinnamon.

¾ cup quinoa

1½ cups water

2 pears or other fresh fruits, chopped

1 handful (about 3 tablespoons) raisins

¾ cup vegetable milk (grain, nut, or soymilk)

3 to 4 tablespoons rice syrup

1 teaspoon ground cinnamon

Banana Cream and Rice Semolina

This breakfast provides a good source of energy to start the day! Quickly prepared, it is made with rice semolina. Treat yourself to this wonderful sweet cream flavored with almond milk.

■ Combine the rice semolina and almond milk in a saucepan. Cook over low heat, stirring constantly, for 5 to 10 minutes, until thickened.

■ Grind the flaxseeds in an electric coffee grinder or dry blender and mix into the cream.

■ Peel and mash the banana with a fork in a large bowl. Add the cream mixture and stir. Depending on the season, I usually complete this cream with a fresh fruit salad and sprinkle it with toasted rice flakes.

⅓ cup rice semolina

1 cup almond milk

1 tablespoon flaxseeds

1 banana

Several spoonfuls toasted rice flakes, raisins, and/or chopped fresh fruit (optional)

Index by Ingredients

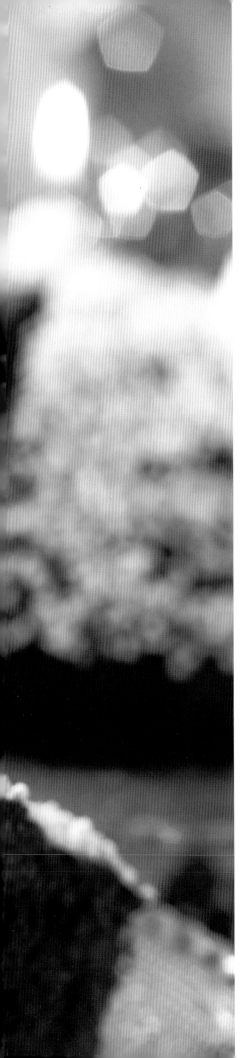